Praise for
Interview Connections

Interviewing great guests and being a guest on other podcasts is by far one of the most successful strategies I've used to grow the Fire Nation community. *Interview Connections* by Jessica Rhodes is a book I highly recommend reading if you want to learn how to get interviewed as a guest, rock your interviews and use the power of podcasting to set your biz ON FIRE!

– John Lee Dumas
Entrepreneur on Fire
www.EoFire.com

Jessica booked spectacular guests for my podcast, *My Kids' Adventures*, and I am thrilled to read all her behind-the-scenes tips in *Interview Connections*. If you want to find and book guests for your podcast who will make you look great, then you need to read this book and learn from Jessica Rhodes!

– Michael Stelzner
Social Media Examiner
www.SocialMediaExaminer.com

Podcasting is one of my top three business-growth tools. Hosting my own podcast sold out my coaching practice to waitlist status. Clients loved my writing, but when they could hear me talk, they connected with me personally and bought. Additionally, being a guest on other people's podcasts builds important relationships with the interviewers, brings your message to new audiences, and builds your site authority. *Interview Connections* will show you how to rock both sides of the mic the right way, so you don't make all the beginner mistakes and can look like a pro from the first word.

– Todd R. Tresidder
Founder & Financial Coach
www.FinancialMentor.com

Jessica Rhodes is the go-to expert when it comes to gaining visibility through podcasting. Her tips and strategies are from her own success as well as the many others she has helped. As a client of Jessica's, I have received so much amazing value and I highly recommend *Interview Connections* for anyone looking to start or grow their podcast as well as for experts looking to get booked. You need to read this book!

– Stacy Tuschl
Mompreneur's Money Map
www.StacyTuschL.com

Forget microphones, RSS feeds, mp3 bit rates, and the rest – without content your podcast is nothing. Great podcasting starts with content. Jessica's talent is in connecting the right talent with the right audiences. This book explains what's really needed, from both sides of the mic, to produce the content your audience is looking for. This is the book the smart people read before they pick up any other book on podcasting.

– Paul Colligan
The Podcast Report
www.PaulColligan.com

Jessica Rhodes covers podcasting from A to Z in *Interview Connections* making it a terrific resource for new and seasoned podcasters alike. Jessica's trustworthy insights and wisdom come from being in the trenches and working her way to success in the podcasting industry, and I have heeded her advice often. Read this book and implement her actionable tips if you want to succeed as a great host, and a rock star guest, as well as leverage your podcast for maximum impact.

– Susie Miller, Author, Consultant, Coach
Founder of The People Skills Lab
www.SusieMiller.com

Interview Connections
How to #ROCKTHEPODCAST From Both Sides of the Mic!

By Jessica Rhodes

Founder of InterviewConnections.com

Interview Connections
How to #ROCKTHEPODCAST From Both Sides of the Mic

Published by Rhodes to Success Publishing
P.O. Box 9664
Warwick, RI 02889

Copyright © 2016 by Entrepreneur Support Services Inc.
All rights reserved. No part of this book may be reproduced, stored in a retrieval system, or transmitted in any form or by any means without the written permission of the publisher.
Printed in the United States of America

ISBN: 978-0998679518

Cover design by Jim Saurbaugh

DISCLAIMER AND/OR LEGAL NOTICES

While the publisher and authors have used their best efforts in preparing this book, they make no representations or warranties with respect to the accuracy or completeness of the contents of this book. The advice and strategies contained herein may not be suitable for your situation. You should consult a professional where appropriate. Neither the publisher nor the authors shall be liable for any loss of profit or any other commercial damages, including but not limited to special, incidental, consequential, or other damages. The purchaser or reader of this publication assumes responsibility for the use of these materials and information. Adherence to all applicable laws and regulations, both advertising and all other aspects of doing business in the United States or any other jurisdiction, is the sole responsibility of the purchaser or reader.

This book is dedicated to my family,
Jamie, Nathan and Lucy.

TABLE OF CONTENTS

Foreword 3

Acknowledgements 5

Preface 7

Getting Started 13

Positioning: The Power of Celebrity 27

Rock the Interview 37

Getting a Return on Your Investment 45

How to Launch and Then Soar 61

Leveraging the Power of Guest Interviews 75

How to Monetize & Market 91

Podcasting to Actually Grow Your Business 115

Resources 135

About the Author – 171

1

FOREWORD

Highly successful entrepreneurs have an insatiable appetite for knowledge, information to help them up-level their personal game, and grow a more profitable business. Over the last few years, the speed and quantity of platforms in which information is shared and consumed seems to grow exponentially.

In the spring of 2012, I launched my podcast, *Stick Like Glue Radio*. I initially took on this additional platform to my marketing because at the time it seemed like the latest trend – and honestly, as a business owner, any time that you can own and effectively control your own media, that's a good thing! And yes, a podcast is a form of media that you own and control.

Little did I know at the time just how powerful this decision would prove to be. My podcast, combined with my busy schedule of being a guest expert on other shows, is hands down one of the most powerful marketing tools I use to grow my business.

I've been blessed with much success as an entrepreneur, and today my primary business is coaching other entrepreneurs in my Dream Business Mastermind and Coaching business. So when my daughter, Jessica (yes, the author of this book!) asked me a few years ago to help her set up a part-time, home-based business, I was excited to do so. Jessica's goal was to earn some extra income to help support her family while still being a stay-at-home mom.

I've always been impressed with Jessica's drive, ambition, and seemingly fearless way she attacked any goal, whether it be acting or working for a nonprofit, effectively selling door to door. I knew her sales skills and tenacity would prove to be valuable assets as an entrepreneur.

One of the services Jessica was providing for me through her VA (virtual assistant) firm was booking me as a guest expert on other podcasts. This was a valuable service for me, and one day

Foreword

while she and I were talking, we came up with a plan to launch this as a separate business… and Interview Connections was born.

In true "Jessica" fashion, she dove in and not only began to grow this business rapidly, she learned as much as she could about the world of podcasting – from both sides of the mic – and has become one of the true recognized leaders in this rapidly growing industry.

When Jessica asked me to write the foreword to this book, I immediately said, "Yes, as your dad and your coach, I would be honored!"

Let me give you my best coaching advice as it relates to podcasting and being a great guest expert: Read this book now – not once, but multiple times!

If you are new to the world of podcasting or are considering starting a podcast or you want to explore being a guest expert on other podcasts, *Interview Connections* is hands down the best book you can read to learn everything you'll need to know to be successful in this arena.

What's truly different about this book is that you'll not only learn the "nuts and bolts" of podcasting, but every chapter also contains truly valuable business-building advice and nuggets of wisdom. So, you'll not only learn how to rock the podcast from both sides of the mic, you'll ultimately learn some powerful strategies to help grow your business.

As I said, read this book cover to cover not just once, but many times!

Jim Palmer
The Dream Business Coach
www.GetJimPalmer.com

ACKNOWLEDGEMENTS

I must start by expressing my sincerest gratitude to my husband, Jamie for supporting me when I said I wanted to be a stay/work-at-home mom and quit my job before I knew how we were going to make ends meet financially. He has never once discouraged me from dreaming and achieving my business ambitions and for that I am eternally grateful.

Thank you to my kids, Nathan and Lucy. The whole reason I started my business was to be a stay-at-home mom, so they are my "why" in business and life. They make me laugh and keep me humble. Thanks, kiddos.

I also want to acknowledge and thank my dad, Jim Palmer, who wrote to you in the foreword of this book. My dad was my first client, and it's because of him saying to me one day, "I want you to book me on podcasts" that I am here writing to you today about podcasting. Thanks, Dad for your support and for always encouraging me to invest in my future growth and profitability!

Thank you to my team of Guest Bookers at Interview Connections. There is no way I could grow my business without the best team on the planet!

Lastly, thank you to my past, present, and future clients at Interview Connections. It's an honor to help you grow your business, leveraging the power of podcasting!

#RockThePodcast!

Jessica Rhodes

Acknowledgements

PREFACE

Promoting yourself and your business is the foundation of marketing. In the late 20th century, doing that meant you had to employ an expensive ad agency or know plenty of people in high places. However, gone are the days when you needed a publishing company to bring a book to market or a studio to bring music to the masses. Technology and the digital revolution changed it all.

The digital age also ushered in your ability to promote yourself "on the air," either as a professional interviewed for your expertise or hosting your own show... previously unthinkable without a fully equipped studio and professional sound editors. You also needed an agent to book you on existing shows and a perhaps a certain level of fame to have your own timeslot. Like I said, technology changed it all. And that's good news for you.

Enter the podcast. Audio broadcasting on the internet. Downloadable files that someone who's interested in what you have to say can listen to anytime, anywhere. It's the "on the air" equivalent of self-published books and indie music. Also gone is the stigma that surrounded those genres in the early days of digital technology. People now realize that simply because a book or song doesn't have the backing of a huge publishing house or studio doesn't make it substandard. Quite the opposite! They're realizing that plenty of people are bringing their talents to the public by themselves and on their own terms... and it's quality stuff.

A podcast enables you to do exactly the same thing. And most importantly, a podcast is a great marketing tool.

I wrote *Interview Connections* to speak to you directly about how to leverage the power of podcasting and podcast interviews to grow your business. There are countless books, courses, blogs, videos, and yes, even podcasts that cover what microphone to use and how to "game the system" in iTunes to get

Preface

your show ranked high. But there is much more to creating a quality podcast so that you get the results you really want.

I'm here to teach you how to leverage the power of podcasting and podcast interviews by focusing on the relationships you will build doing them! Perhaps you're thinking that podcasting isn't really for you, and if so, you're wrong. Consumers aren't looking for marketing. We're all inundated with marketing and advertising all day long and at every turn, and most people have become very adept at tuning out advertising. Instead, consumers are looking for content: useful information that helps them solve a problem and is entertaining. Content is at the heart of podcasting.

Content is king in the world of marketing, and podcasting is all about providing useful content that consumers want!

Imagine your prospects and customers on the drive to work. They'll be exposed to a certain amount of advertising: a billboard here for five seconds or a 30-second commercial on the radio. You've no doubt experienced it yourself. Both are expensive and gone in five to 30 seconds. Now imagine your prospects and customers listening to a 20- to 30-minute podcast... and specifically looking forward to doing so!

Like I said, podcasting is a fantastic tool, and it is not beyond your grasp or budget.

Podcasting in general and this book specifically is for you if you...

- Are an entrepreneur with a thriving business.
- Know and understand that you should *always* be marketing.
- Want to leverage the power of podcasting as either a guest or a host, but don't want to make it your new full-time gig.

Interview Connections

- Are in it for the long haul. Podcasting is a powerful marketing strategy, but it is *not* a quick fix for a struggling business.

So dive in to this book now and get ready to *#ROCKTHEPODCAST From Both Sides of the Mic!*

Preface

PART 1:
ROCK THE PODCAST AS A GUEST EXPERT

CHAPTER ONE:
GETTING STARTED

First things first: Why would you even want to consider or pursue being interviewed on a podcast? Simply, it's all about exposure. If you're in business for yourself, you are undoubtedly very good at what you do. I'll even go so far as to say you're an expert. Why not promote your expertise?

The answer is easy: Your prospects and customers will buy from you for that very reason – your expertise. Your knowledge and experience set you apart from your competition. Whatever your product or service may be, you want to be unsurpassed in your field… and you want your prospects and clients to know that.

It's one thing to proclaim your own expertise in your marketing materials, but it's quite another to demonstrate it and let prospects and customers come to that conclusion by themselves.

Consider yourself as the consumer. You see an ad proclaiming that Joe Smith is the smartest financial consultant around. Of course, you take that with a grain of salt. Joe Smith bought the advertising space (whether it's in print, on the internet, or on the air), so why would Joe Smith say anything else about himself other than something positive and glowing? Sure, you can try to dig deeper and uncover more about Joe Smith either by asking around or trying to discern testimonials and similar information about him.

Now, imagine you hear Joe Smith being interviewed on the podcast you listen to about personal finance. He discusses the latest trends and the impacts of changing markets. Joe offers sound advice regarding balancing your portfolio and tips on boosting your savings and investments. Yes, Joe is still talking about himself; however, the podcast host is there to ask verifying questions and prod Joe for more information. A good interviewer will keep the discussion more objective. A good podcast host will not allow the interview to become a promotion. As you listen, it's obvious that Joe is smart and really does know his stuff. Based on your own conclusion after listening to him, you are far more likely to hire Joe as your financial consultant! It has far more impact on you than his advertisement that simply proclaimed Joe to be the best.

When you are a guest expert on a podcast, you have the same opportunity. You can discuss your expertise and answer questions to demonstrate that you really do know your stuff and you have the ability to solve listeners' problems and provide them with what they want or need. What you have to say is the content they're looking for rather than another advertisement.

Their Podcast, Their Rules

Now that I've helped you understand *why* you want to be a guest on a podcast, let's talk about some of the *hows*, including equipment, sound quality, and steps to be a great interviewee.

Quality matters. Yes, what you have to say – the content – matters, but quality also goes beyond the information you share. As I mentioned in the preface, technology now allows anyone to be a published author, a musician with recorded songs, and an expert guest on a podcast. However, that author, musician, and guest expert have to bring their "A games." If the book isn't well written and the story captivating or if the song is awful, no one is going to read or buy. The same is true for the podcast. Your host wants quality sound on the show or listeners tune out.

If you have great content, your audience will forgive poor sound quality. But if you are a guest expert with poor sound quality, a host will NOT forgive you.

When it's your show, you set the standards with the audience. Your listeners will become accustomed to and love your show for what it is. In fact, I have one client who has been podcasting for over four years and records the show on a conference call line. He and the guests call in with their telephones, and the podcast, while clear, sounds like AM radio. Because he's been delivering amazing content week after week for years on end, his audience doesn't care if it sounds like AM radio! They know what to expect on his podcast because he's been consistent and focuses on the content rather than the sound. So... his podcast, his rules.

But – and this is a really *big* but – when you're the guest on a podcast, you have to play by the host's rules. In the case of my client, it would be okay to call in on the conference line and sound like AM radio because that is his standard. But not everyone plays by those rules. You need to understand and play by the host's rules. After all, it's their game. They're setting the standard and know what their audience expects and wants.

If a host records over Skype, you'd better download and install Skype on your computer and use a microphone with headphones. If the host records on a conference call line, brush the dust off your landline and call in on time. I can't stress this enough: Their podcast, their rules!

In addition to how you record with your host, there may also be expectations regarding content. In marketing, content is king, especially in the realm of blogs and podcasts. Some hosts will have very specific questions, and they want you to be prepared to answer them while others prefer to keep their podcasts conversational. The host knows their audience. It is your job as the guest to be prepared to add value to support the show's format. Do your homework and listen to previous episodes to get a flavor of the tone and show flow. You don't want to come off as stuffy on a comedic show, and you don't want to sound shallow on a show with a more serious, professional tone.

Getting Started

Podcast hosts are very protective of their shows because they want to deliver the most valuable content possible to their listeners. As a guest, you have a responsibility to add to the podcast, not detract from their quality of the production. As we continue through this chapter, I'll teach you the basics to get started as a guest expert for podcasts, so you have the equipment, web presence, and messaging needed to add value to every podcast that books you for an interview.

But before we jump into that, there's a simple professional courtesy you should follow. When you receive an email or other contact inviting you to be a guest, reply promptly! Failure to do so may lead the host to believe you're not really interested in being on the show. Don't let one, two, or three days go by before you even acknowledge the invitation to be on the show. First of all, it's rude to not express your gratitude! Next, it doesn't reflect well on your organizational abilities, and the host may already be worrying about your reliability to call in on time for the interview. Even if you aren't certain about your schedule, simply respond with an acknowledgement of receiving the invitation, thank them, and tell them that you will reply to schedule within a certain time frame (e.g. in two days, end of the week, etc.). Be easy to work with and ask, "What else do you need?" Ensure that you're not exhibiting "diva-like" tendencies with focus on you rather than trying to make the show a success. And, once again, say "thank you"!

Occasionally you may need to reschedule an interview due to unforeseen circumstances, but remember that if you have a podcast interview scheduled and at the last minute you cancel and request to reschedule, it sends the message that the interview is not a priority to you. It reflects poorly on you, so view podcast interview appearances as important meetings and don't cancel if at all possible.

Rock one podcast as a guest and you'll find other shows beating a path to your door to book you as well.

Equipment

Just because you may not host your own podcast does not mean you don't need good equipment. If you plan to get booked as a guest expert on podcasts to grow your business, you need to invest in some basic tools to contribute the best sound possible to each recording.

Remember the client I mentioned whose podcast sounds like AM radio? I assure you, he's more the exception than the rule. Sound quality *Smartphones are useful for almost everything – except recording a podcast. Use your computer for the call, not your phone and your host will appreciate it!* matters, and poor sound quality will often turn off listeners (and I mean that literally and figuratively) no matter what is being discussed or how great the topic may be. Poor sound quality can be a distraction, and even worse, can suggest poor content quality to those tuning in for the first time. We're all a bit time crunched, and no one wants to waste time trying to glean useful information from a poor sounding podcast.

A lot of podcast hosts and guests today connect by either Skype or Zoom. When you're booked for an interview, the host will clarify which application they use and that will be your cue to ensure that the software is downloaded and installed on your Mac or PC. (TIP: If they do NOT provide this information, reach out to the host ASAP to ask how the interview will be recorded. You'll gain points with them immediately by demonstrating that you're going to be a pro and add to the value of their podcast.)

Even though both Skype and Zoom can be used on a smartphone, you should be using them on your computer in a quiet space. Background noise is distracting. And test the platform before your scheduled call! You want to be certain you know what

Getting Started

you're doing, or you risk looking like a rookie, which can get the podcast off to a terrible start – for both you and the host.

While your computer may have a built-in microphone, do NOT rely on this microphone for your podcast interviews! You'll be plagued with echo, sounds delays, and your recording will not sound good at all. My friend, Corey Coates, co-owner of Podfly Productions can talk to you for hours about all the different kinds of microphones, mixers, USB interfaces and more, but as you're getting started, I'm going to keep this very simple for you.

As you're reading this book and considering being a guest expert for podcasts (and as we've just covered the importance of sound quality), you want to sound good on a podcast, but you probably don't necessarily care about super fancy equipment. I suggest you order the ATR 2100 microphone on Amazon, and for less than a hundred bucks, you'll sound better than most guests out there.

Also, be sure you know how to mute the microphone you use. When you feel a cough coming on, a quick mute can pre-empt that distracting cough. And go ahead and practice muting and unmuting yourself before the interview.

If you're really craving some technical information, allow me to take a moment to satisfy that craving. A condenser microphone (like the Blue Yeti) is good if you have a studio that is extremely quiet because it will pick up all sound in the room. A dynamic microphone (like the ATR 2100) is best for most podcasters recording from home or in their office because it will just pick up your voice – the sound right in front of it. So cars driving by and cats meowing outside your door won't be heard.

A condenser mic tends to be more sensitive and accurate while a dynamic mic is typically more durable and can deliver consistent sound quality in almost every situation. If you're considering a condenser mic, Blue Yeti is a solid choice.

Okay... back to non-techy talk!

Sound Quality & Your Space

Now that you know what kind of microphone to use and that you should be on a computer rather than a smartphone, let's talk about your space. Podcasts are not radio shows recorded in sound-proof studios (unless you are a "pro-caster"!), and they're not drive-by interviews with the local news in which the listener expects to hear background noise. Most podcasts require a quiet space, so the listener is hearing the content and the content alone... not anything in the background.

As soon as the listener hears Mike the landscaper mowing your lawn, the mood is ruined, the listener may tune out, and your host won't be pleased! Record your interview in a quiet, carpeted room at a time when you will not have interruptions. Close the door!

You can discuss the best times to record with your host since the podcast isn't a live broadcast. Perhaps the best time for you will be in the afternoon while the baby is napping or in the evening after everyone in the house has gone to bed. Your host will likely work with you to determine the best mutually beneficial time for the interview.

Turn your cell phone off or put it on airplane mode and also ensure that your desk phone (if you have one) is muted or unplugged. Also, put Skype on Do Not Disturb. In addition to eliminating a potential sound disturbance, you don't want these interruptions to derail your train of thought while you're answering a question!

There are also steps to take with your computer before you begin the recorded interview, especially if you are using Skype. Even Apple's highest end iMac with a brand new version of Skype can experience technical difficulties. Before your scheduled interview, re-start your computer and re-start Skype. Shut down all other applications, and if you can, use a hard-wired internet connection as opposed to Wi-Fi alone.

Last but not least, make sure your microphone is plugged in, your headphones are on, and you double check your settings to ensure that your computer is picking up your sound from your external microphone and not your computer's internal microphone.

Web Presence

So now you have a good microphone, a quiet room, and valuable information to contribute to a podcast. You've restarted your computer and tested the connections and sound quality. You're good to go, right? Not so fast. Those factors, while critically important, do not add up to you being the perfect guest.

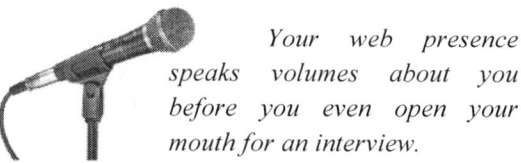

Your web presence speaks volumes about you before you even open your mouth for an interview.

We're living in an online world, so a listener's first impression of you is often your website or social media profiles. They may Google you at the start of the podcast or even in advance if the host has previously promoted your interview. Depending on what they find, they may or may not choose to download your episode.

When a podcaster interviews you on their show, they are giving you a tacit endorsement in front of their audience. If you give a great interview, the listener will likely visit your website and/or follow you on Facebook, Twitter or LinkedIn... certainly the results you want! If your website is poorly designed and provides no value, that can reflect poorly on the host who interviewed you. What are you posting on social media sites? Are you posting positive updates, sharing helpful articles, and leaving nice comments, or are you posting angry rants and complaints and sharing the latest political controversy? The latter of which is a poor reflection on you *and* on the host who included you on their podcast.

Interview Connections

To be a great guest and get booked for interviews, you need to take a close look at your online presence. In fact, your potential host will very likely research you online before even booking you. If they don't like what they see (poorly designed, useless site... or no site at all and/or inappropriate comments on social media), they'll very likely pass on booking you as a guest no matter what level of expertise you might bring to the table and share with their audience.

At Interview Connections, we look for personal branding for potential guests before we even agree to represent them. You have to represent yourself as an expert in your area if you want to get booked on podcasts. We also review your site for broken links and poor navigation. If these exist, it's a problem because it reflects sloppiness on your part, and that's certainly not what podcasters are looking for!

Make sure you are presenting yourself online in the most positive light possible. I am not saying you need to be fake, but before you post anything online, ask yourself, "Will this make someone smile or provide value in some way?" If not and you feel you must absolutely express the thought, write it in your journal... your paper journal that only you see.

One Sheet

Those who are regularly interviewed in traditional media outlets most likely have a media kit, containing the pertinent information the interviewer should know, so the interview comes off professionally and worth watching.

A media or press kit contains your bio, facts about your business, media contact information, and promotional photos of you, your book or whatever you are... promoting! It has the exact information that a news outlet or event coordinator needs from a presenter or interviewee. If you're trying to get a ton of press, then a press release and media kit are the right things to have!

However, if you want to get interviewed on podcasts, I discourage you from sending podcasters a press release or media kit because, quite frankly, it does not send the right message. Notice its contents: "This is who I am; this is my latest book; this is something I want to promote and get a lot of press for" is all "I" or egocentric language where it's all about what *you* want. You don't want to talk about what you want when you are trying to get booked for podcast interviews. You need to talk about what the *audience* will gain from hearing your interview.

The message you need to send a podcaster is that you will bring immense value to their audience. Why else would they be booking you in the first place? When I train new booking agents who work at Interview Connections, I teach them to write the following in their pitches to podcasters: "My client would be a great guest for your show because <fill in the blank>." What follows after "because" is the crux of it all. It represents the content the guest will share. When we represent entrepreneurs, authors, and speakers to get them booked on podcasts, our strategy is to demonstrate to podcast hosts how our client's content will be valuable to their listeners. Again, if the interviewee is bringing nothing but self-promotion to the podcast, why conduct the interview? The audience will be getting nothing more than long-winded advertising.

In addition to a well-written pitch by your booking agent, a podcaster should also receive from you a "one sheet" that presents you as a guest expert. A one sheet is a document (ideally a PDF for easy sharing) that is designed to match your branding and includes the following information:

- Your headshot*
- Your bio written in the third person (Should be one to two paragraphs, so the host can read it as an introduction to the show.)
- Suggested interview questions and/or interview topics

- Your contact information: your email, phone number, Skype ID, and mailing address

(*A few notes about your headshot: You need to look professional! When you're a guest expert, you become a brand ambassador for the podcast. A bad headshot reflects poorly on the host and the show by association. Your headshot says a lot about you, so you also want to ensure your headshot matches your brand and signals how you conduct your business. It must also be an honest representation of you or you're immediately building a level of distrust.)

Your one sheet will do the same work as a media kit, but with the right tone and tenor: underscoring the value you will contribute to the podcast. It will demonstrate your professionalism before you even open your mouth.

Be sure your bio isn't too short or too long. If it's too short, the host won't have enough information to ascertain whether or not you're credible and a good fit for the podcast. If it's too long, the host may not read it. Three to five sentences is ideal and should highlight those aspects of your professional life that showcase you as the ideal guest expert for the podcast you're pitching. Spotlight the relevant parts of your personality, expertise, and interest.

It's your job to demonstrate how your content is valuable and relevant to the podcast audience. If the show is weekly, you need to convince the host that you are one of the top 52 professionals in your industry!

Get Started!

Being a guest on a podcast is an easier introduction to podcasting than launching your own show. You don't have to edit the podcast, worry about maintaining a schedule, do the marketing, or submit an RSS feed to iTunes. (A what? My point, exactly.) Getting started in podcasting as a guest expert is the perfect way to "put your toe in the water" to test this platform as a potential marketing strategy for you and your business.

However, don't let that statement mislead you. Successfully leveraging the power of being a guest expert requires a long-term investment and work. You have to do your homework and be prepared even before you contact a booking agent.

Before you move on to the next chapter, go to Amazon right now and order your microphone (remember what I recommended: the ATR 2100, a dynamic microphone!), download Skype, and have some professional headshots taken. In the next chapter, I'll teach you the power of celebrity and how to position yourself as one, so podcast hosts request you as a guest!

#ROCKTHEPODCAST Recap:

- *Technology has enabled every entrepreneur to promote their expertise without needing a PR person or an expensive studio.*

- *When you're invited to be interviewed for a podcast, rule #1 is: their podcast, their rules.*

- *The podcast host sets the bar for sound quality and they want it to be good... with a very rare exception.*

- *Invest in a quality microphone, and ask what platform the podcast host uses (likely Skype or Zoom).*

- *Ensure you have a quiet space in which to be recorded for the interview and don't rely on a smartphone. Close the door!*

- *Ensure you have a web presence that both you and the host can be proud of. By interviewing you, your host is providing tacit endorsement of you.*

- *Create a one sheet that explains who you are and most importantly, what value you will bring to the podcast. It's about the value the audience gets from the interview, not about whatever it may be that you want to promote.*

Getting Started

CHAPTER TWO:
POSITIONING: THE POWER OF CELEBRITY

Okay. So I just told you that being interviewed on a podcast is a great way to market by developing relationships and demonstrating your expertise as well as being a great way for you to test the waters of podcasting. You also now have the right equipment to record podcast interviews (you bought that mic like I told you, right?), your sound quality is tip top, you have a nice website and social media presence, and you have a one sheet. You're ready to go, but there's still a big question. How do you get podcasters interested in interviewing you, so you can show off your expertise and put all those things to work?

The answer is positioning and the power of celebrity.

Remember how the digital age ushered in the ability to publish your own books, record your own songs, and create your own "on air" presence? It also did something else. We live in this amazing time in which you can create your own celebrity persona almost overnight. And guess what? That's exactly what podcasters want: the ability to align themselves with successful entrepreneurs and celebrities.

Of course, if you get a starring role in a movie or TV show, write and record a killer song, or win a gold medal, you're going to become a celebrity, mostly because of how our culture views actors, musicians, and athletes and bestows celebrity status upon them. In business, however, entrepreneurs become celebrities because they position themselves as such. They understand the importance of self-promotion of their areas of expertise.

In the online marketing world, "celebrity" is all about perception. It has nothing to do with how much money you have,

Positioning: The Power of Celebrity

the number of names on your email list, or the size of your social media following. Anyone can position themselves as a celebrity, and it is a very smart business strategy because people are attracted to celebrities and will pay you more money for your products or services if they perceive you to be a celebrity.

You are already an expert in your particular field. That expertise is either the reason you started your business, or it has grown and developed with experience since you launched your enterprise. Now you want to become the go-to authority by creating your own celebrity.

Celebrity status is no longer only for famous actors, musicians, and athletes. The business world is filled with celebrity entrepreneurs who are the go-to authorities in their respective niches.

I'll share something with you. My business coach is Jim Palmer, "The Dream Business Coach." Jim also happens to be my dad, so I know him pretty well. When I started my business, I certainly didn't think he was a celebrity! (Truth be told, I still don't personally view him as one, but sshhhh... that secret is between you and me.) However, after I joined his Dream Business Coaching and Mastermind Program, I came to understand from him and other successful entrepreneurs the power of positioning and celebrity.

Entrepreneur celebrities are viewed as the go-to authorities in their respective niches. That authority is founded in their expertise – expertise that they promote!

In the case of my dad, his first business was a done-for-you newsletter marketing company, and one day, after a client experienced a great deal of success with his newsletter, he said to my dad, "You're the newsletter guru!" From that day on, my dad became known as "Jim Palmer, The Newsletter Guru." It became the tag line that he used in all of his marketing. It became his position and celebrity.

My dad isn't the only entrepreneur to use this strategy. My good friend and mentor, Susie Miller, is a relationship expert who works with married entrepreneurs – couples who work together in their own business. She refers to them as "Entre-Spouses," and as you can imagine, being married and running a business together can present a whole new set of challenges in a relationship. Susie has a long, successful history offline as a marriage counselor, and in September 2014, she started her journey in bringing her business online and to more couples. She branded herself as "The *better* Relationship Coach, equipping folks to build *better* relationships in 30 days or less!"

Next, Susie authored a best-selling, traditionally published book, *Listen, Learn, Love: How to Dramatically Improve Your Relationships in 30 Days or Less!* She positioned herself as a celebrity expert for entrepreneurs who are married to each other and run their businesses together. As a result, Susie continues to sell out her coaching programs and is sought after as a guest expert for podcasts.

Yes, You Are a Celebrity

So, how do you position yourself as a celebrity? It's very easy: Just call yourself one! Jim didn't go to "newsletter marketing college" to earn a degree that came with the title Newsletter Guru. Susie didn't compete with her peers and win the title of being better than the rest. They both simply positioned themselves as the guru and the better coach.

While I assert it's easy – and it is – the underlying factor is expertise. You have to have it. Yes, Jim could call himself a guru, just as anyone could, but that positioning would not have gained traction if he didn't know what he was talking about or if newsletters are not the great marketing tool he purports them to be. The same is true for Susie. While she has a very defined niche in

Positioning: The Power of Celebrity

working with married-to-each-other entrepreneurs, she also has a track record that supports her branding as "the *better* Relationship Coach."

Do you have a successful track record and are you an expert in your niche? I'm certain you are or you would not be reading this book! So on to creating your own celebrity because, yes, you are a celebrity.

The only way people will believe you are a celebrity, though, is if you are consistently and persistently marketing and delivering your value and that message to your tribe. More likely than not, entrepreneurs who are positioned as celebrities have their own podcasts, video shows, blogs, newsletters (email, print, or both), and attend and network or present at live events or conferences. I speak from experience. If you consistently publish weekly podcasts, videos, blogs, emails, and attend live events, you will start to feel the power of celebrity impact your business in a major way.

Consistency and persistence pay off in creating your celebrity status. Use your blog, newsletters, and attendance at live events to promote your expertise... and hence, your celebrity status.

Let's take a moment to think about celebrity actors and musicians again. The first time they appear on a screen or stage, few people know who they are. Their talent does all the talking. Like your expertise, they have to have talent or they don't appear in another movie, TV show, or concert again. Over time, they become more and more recognizable because of the consistency of their appearance along with the display of their talent. They become sought-after celebrities. Think about any of the TV shows that are talent competitions. The participants who bomb are done; the ones

Interview Connections

with talent move on to the next round. By the end of the competition, the winner is a celebrity.

Celebrity – whether it's for an actor, musician, athlete, or you – does not happen overnight. In fact, it doesn't necessarily happen in six months or a year. But consistently continue to plug yourself, and you will start meeting people who act a little star struck. They'll recognize you! At the very least, they'll think or say, "Oh yeah, he's the one who's the Newsletter Guru." Or "She's the better Relationship Coach." Or "Wow, you're the one who <insert your own promoted expertise here>!"

It's a strange thing I must admit because, personally, I don't think I'm a celebrity. However, when I get on a podcast as a guest expert and say hello to the host for the first time, it dawns on me that they've been watching my videos, listening to my own podcasts, and seeing my posts on social media. When they finally meet me, there is that element of, "Whoa! I'm really talking to you in person!"

Creating celebrity is pretty much the same as any other advertising. There's a product that works great and, in order for it to be in demand and create success for its inventor, consumers have to know what it is, what it does, and that it works great. The only way this happens is through consistent promotion and branding. So now there's a product – you – and what you do helps solve problems for your prospects and customers and you're an expert at what you do. You get the results people want. The only way to be in demand is to create celebrity with consistent promotion and branding.

Get the Celebrity Ball Rolling

Think about the examples I shared about Jim Palmer and Susie Miller. They both determined their respective niches and built their celebrity on that. That's what you'll need to answer for yourself. Take a moment to consider and answer these brainstorming questions:

- What's your niche?
- What do people know you for?
- What is your area of expertise?
- What problem(s) do you solve for your clients?
- What sets you apart from your competition?
- How do you see yourself?
- What do you want to be known for?
- What compliments regarding your skill and expertise have clients paid you? (Think about that one customer telling Jim Palmer he was a "newsletter guru.")
- When you are the guest expert on a podcast, what value will you bring to listeners?

In getting the celebrity ball rolling, you have to make some investments. Presentation matters. Invest in your branding and work with professional graphic and website designers. Don't skimp. Don't get the cheapest freelancer you might find on Fiverr.com or similar platform, and certainly (unless you *are* a graphic designer or website specialist) don't try to do it yourself. Shoddy or unprofessional work will immediately undermine the celebrity you are working to create for yourself.

Get referrals from trusted advisors, colleagues, or fellow entrepreneurs and be prepared to give your wallet a bit of a workout. I'm not suggesting that you have to go broke in developing your brand and marketing pieces that support it, but remember: you get what you pay for! I invested a lot in re-branding my blog, podcast, TV show, social media presence, and website, and it has been paying dividends. As an entrepreneur, you surely understand that you have to invest money to make money, and the same mindset applies here.

(As a side note, I recommend contacting Lindsey Anderson at TrafficandLeads.com. I've worked with her, and she designed my site, InterviewConnections.com.)

Business celebrities are the go-to resources and authority figures, so the next thing for you to do after creating a professional-looking branding presence is to begin expanding your celebrity persona on social media, and that goes well beyond your own Facebook, LinkedIn, and other social media pages and profiles.

Look for groups on social media sites that attract your target market. For example, if you're a landscaper, look for pages and groups where those interested in gardening hang out. Begin answering questions in on those sites and in forums to show that you're an expert. Comment strategically on posts where you can offer value. Don't simply promote yourself. Be sure you are adding value. As with podcasting as a marketing tool, this type of exposure is about showing that you are the expert and building relationships.

As I mentioned before: Never, ever be negative or use social media as a place to vent or complain. Successful entrepreneurs do not cloud the air with negativity. Additionally, while you are the expert, when answering questions, be cognizant of tempering your language to avoid coming off as a "know-it-all." No one likes a know-it-all, but everyone appreciates an expert.

While you might have considered yourself to be an expert in your niche, perhaps you never thought of yourself as a celebrity. In truth, those are essentially two sides of the same coin… but you have to position and promote yourself as the celebrity that you are! Do that and you will find podcast hosts seeking you out as a guest expert.

One of the best ways to position yourself as a celebrity is to hire a team. You probably already have a team who handles certain aspects of your business like accounting, taxes, web design, etc., so why not use a team to create and promote your celebrity? If you are pitching podcasters yourself, you are **not** positioning yourself as a celebrity. Think about any celebrity. They have teams, and celebrities live and work behind gates – either literal or figurative ones.

Celebrities use others to handle their bookings for them for two very good reasons. First, they do it to enhance and underscore their celebrity status. They also outsource the booking process because they're smart entrepreneurs and understand the value of their time. Their best return on investment occurs when they focus on their core competency and running their business. Their time is worth far more than what they would pay someone else to book and schedule interviews.

Check out how Interview Connections can help you boost your celebrity status by getting you booked on podcasts as a guest expert and handing all of the scheduling details.

#ROCKTHEPODCAST Recap:

- *The digital age brought about the ability to create your own celebrity persona. You no longer have to be famous by 20th century standards to gain recognition.*

- *Entrepreneurial celebrities are viewed as the go-to authorities in their respective niches.*

- *You can establish yourself as a celebrity simply by stating that you are one… and backing it up with your expertise.*

- *Your celebrity status will only gain traction if you consistently and persistently deliver that message and make it part of your branding and marketing.*

- *Celebrity status doesn't happen overnight. As with any type of advertising, it takes time and it takes repetition.*

- *Don't skimp on the presentation of your brand. Hire professionals and be prepared to spend money to make money.*

- *Look at social media groups and forums as a place to share your expertise and build your celebrity.*

Positioning: The Power of Celebrity

CHAPTER THREE:
ROCK THE INTERVIEW

So far we've covered what you need to know to rock the podcast as a guest expert: the equipment, your space, web presence, one sheet, and your position as a celebrity. Now it's time to make sure you rock the interviews and turn hosts and listeners into leads for your business!

When you're a guest expert on a podcast, there are several small things you should do before the recording to ensure a high quality show:

- Close all applications and re-start your computer. Whether you're recording on a mobile device or the highest end iMac, you run the risk of dropping the call if you do not close all other applications and re-start your machine. Dropping the call is akin to a cardinal sin.

- Use the bathroom and get a glass of water. It sounds like a silly suggestion, or rather a suggestion for a 5-year-old, but the last distraction you need during the interview is thinking about how much you have to pee! You'll be speaking at length, so drinking water will keep you hydrated and help you speak more clearly and give you a natural energy boost.

- Is it winter? Kill the space heater. Summer? Turn off fans and air conditioning. You would be surprised how much background noise those appliances make! Background noises *kill* sound quality and listeners (and the host!) will not forgive you for it.

- Before connecting, stand up, touch your toes, then reach for the sky – stretch out! By getting your blood flowing and having your body stretched, you'll have more energy and a more noticeable pep in your voice, and listeners will then be more engaged in what you have to say.

- Write the host's name and attach it to your monitor. This will serve as a reminder to use their name throughout the interview.

- Last but not least: Don't be late! One minute before the recording, send a message to the host: "Ready when you are!"

My biggest recommendation and tip for rocking the podcast is to exhibit only the best communication and speaking skills. Do your homework and review what topics you want to cover and the points you want to make. And practice, practice, practice! You may even want to role play with a friend or family member in the role of the host and record the discussion you have. Listen to it to uncover your crutch words – the "ums," "yeahs," etc. We all have them, and while a podcast is conversational (unlike a prepared speech), you want your speaking skills to shine rather than become a distraction.

Use the host's name throughout the conversation. When I'm interviewing guests on *Rhodes to Success*, I make a point to use their name in questions. It makes them feel good and it's easy to do. For example, "That's a great question, Jessica, I'm glad you asked." "Well, Jessica, here's how I approach that issue...." Having the host's name posted on your monitor is a great way to prompt yourself to remember to use it. Obviously, you don't want to overdo it! "Well, Jessica, as I mentioned earlier, Jessica, the strategy I used, Jessica, was to...." You get the idea.

Next, your number one goal as a guest expert on a podcast is to make the host look good. That's right. When you are the guest expert, you are there to bring value to that podcast and help make the host look good to their audience. Remember, it isn't about you and your own self-promotion. Marketing your business through podcasting is about building relationships. There's no better way to build a relationship than by making someone else look good.

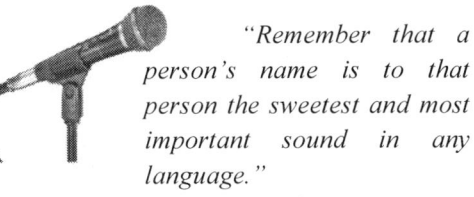

> *"Remember that a person's name is to that person the sweetest and most important sound in any language."*
> *~ Dale Carnegie*

How do you go about it? Start by researching the show and learning about the host's background prior to the interview. Discover what their business is and the products or services they sell. In your answers, you can give them a plug and help them promote their own business to their listeners.

I suspect that sounds very counterintuitive to you, but let me share a really great example of how this can work to your advantage. When I interviewed Matt Miller (an Air Force veteran who bought one gumball machine and turned it into a franchise business: School Spirit Vending for year-round school fundraising), he very generously gave Interview Connections a huge plug.

Matt said, "If you are a business owner looking to promote your business, the first thing you need to do immediately is contact Jessica's team at Interview Connections and work with them. I am one of their clients and have been for a number of months. I started out doing all this podcast stuff on my own, and I still do some on my own because it's that important, but to have her team working on my behalf to find additional shows that my message fits with and make that introduction to where I literally just have to show up is huge because I have so many plates that are spinning at any one time. Their expertise and advice is invaluable."

I don't mean to be Captain Obvious here, but how much do you think I promote Matt Miller's interview compared to some other episodes? Spoiler alert: *A lot!*

Because Matt so generously promoted my business during his interview, I promote that episode regularly, and in turn, Matt gets a ton of exposure because he's the featured expert on the show. Oh, and I also gave him a big feature right here in this book because of his generosity!

Adding Value for the Audience

In addition to making the host look good, you can provide a ton of value to the audience (and drive traffic to your own website or a landing page) by making a free offer at the end of the interview. When you make a free offer, you are encouraging the listener to take action and visit your site. The free offer should have a high perceived value. It can be more information for the listeners regarding the topic of the show or something that helps them take action to fulfill a need or want based on the interview.

However, this "call to action" must be crystal clear. What exactly are you offering to the listener if they visit your site? Is the value clearly defined? If it's a special report or giveaway of some sort, does it clearly relate to the value that you've just shared during the podcast?

You must also be very clear about what you want and then be specific with listeners about the action you want them to take. I was recently speaking with a client who's been a guest expert on podcasts for several months. When I asked him about his progress, he said, "Podcasts are going well. I'm getting good feedback, but I'm not quite getting the results I want."

So I asked him what his desired results were. He said, "I have a free e-book that I want listeners to download, and I would also like more Twitter followers."

My follow-up question? "Are you telling listeners to download that e-book and are you telling people to connect with you on Twitter?"

He was not doing that because he was worried about coming off as too sales-y. You'll recall that earlier in the book I strongly advised you to avoid self-promotion as a guest expert on podcasts. I whole-heartedly stick by that, but having a clear call to action is not being sales-y or self-promotional because you aren't **selling** anything. Remember, it's a free offer. You're not offering a paid program or paid service. You're offering something of value for free.

Provide a valuable free offer and specifically tell listeners what they need to do to get it. Do those things and you'll get the results you want as a guest expert on podcasts.

My recommendation to this client and to you if you're really worried about it is to ask the host before the show or even during the recording, "I have a free e-book that I would love to offer your listeners as a gift. Is it okay if I do that?" I can't imagine any podcast host who would say no, and if it turns out that they really have a problem with it, they'll tell you (or edit it out of the show).

Give a strong call to action. You can't expect listeners to take action on something you don't ask them to do, and your call to action must be strong. When I think of strength, I picture someone who is confident, sure of themselves, who cannot be easily walked over, and knows the value they have and offer and whose purpose is not up for debate. When you think about your call to action, is it irresistible? When delivering your call to action, does your tone communicate that you know, without a doubt, that your offer **will** help the listener?

Whatever it may be, your call to action has to be easy to understand and communicate. Think: One step! There should only be one thing the listener needs to do to get the benefit. Do not ask listeners to visit such-and-such website, then go to the associated social media page, and then send an email to get whatever's being offered. One step! Give them one clear, single instruction that they should act on.

In all likelihood, that call to action will be to visit a website. If that site's URL is really long, create a succinct, easy-to-remember link that shortens it. Keep in mind that listeners may be driving, walking, working out at the gym, or otherwise without the opportunity to take notes while listening.

My client, Heather Havenwood, uses SMS marketing for her call to action, so instead of giving a URL to type into a web browser, she tells listeners to text a single word to a 5-digit number. There are many services that offer this. I took Heather's advice and signed up with Mobit.com, so now I can have listeners text the word "Rock" to 72000, and that directs them to a landing page on the mobile web browser.

Your call to action has to be easy to remember. And repeat it. If you doubt the importance of repetition, listen to any radio or television advertisement that communicates a phone number. It's repeated and repeated and repeated. There's a reason for that! Make sure your URL is easy to remember and repeat it.

Post-interview Steps

Once the recording is over, you still have opportunities to market through relationship building. The host will most likely invite you for a few minutes of chit chat once you're off the air. Use this time very wisely.

My business coach, Jim Palmer (and you'll remember, he is also my dad!) has literally done hundreds of interviews both as a guest expert and a host. When he is interviewed by a new podcaster, they will sometimes ask him for feedback. He wisely uses this time at the end of the recording to give them some coaching. The host greatly appreciates the advice, and it shows off what a great coach Jim is! This also opens the door for Jim to invite them to his live event, Dream Business Academy, attendees of which almost always convert to coaching clients, adding thousands of dollars to his yearly revenue.

Next, after your call with the host ends, don't forget to show your gratitude. Send a thank-you card or gift to the host. This keeps you on their radar and makes you stand out and be remembered.

I was interviewed by Mary Kathryn Johnson on her podcast, *Parent Entrepreneur Success*, and during the interview, we discussed how much we both love coffee. The next day I purchased a one-pound bag of coffee from a local shop near my home in Rhode Island and sent it to her via USPS priority mail. Making this type of investment of my time and money strengthened my relationship with Mary, and I know thanking her for spotlighting me will pay dividends in the future.

Even if you don't choose to send a gift, send a thank-you note – a snail-mailed thank you. In this day and age of emails and texts, a note that arrives in envelope in someone's mailbox really stands out. And never underestimate the power of a snail-mailed card!

My client, Josh Latimer, created SendJim.com, an app that makes sending thank-you cards and gifts super easy! SendOutCards.com is another solution for simple card and gift sending.

There is no excuse for not getting this done. It's an easy way to continue to build the relationship and leverage the interview that's already been recorded.

Remember: Podcast marketing is not about slimy tactics and gaming iTunes ranking algorithm. It's about relationships! Committing to a great show, being a giver and making the host look good, and focusing on what you can offer the host and listeners will, above all, else really help you rock the podcast as a guest expert!

#ROCKTHEPODCAST Recap:

- ❖ *Ensure that your technology is ready to go before starting. Close all applications and re-start your computer.*

- ❖ *Be sure your body is ready to go – use the bathroom and get a drink of water. Do some stretching and moving before you start to boost your energy level. That comes through in your voice and will keep listeners engaged.*

- ❖ *Practice, practice, practice. Record a test interview as a role playing exercise and listen for any crutch words you may have.*

- ❖ *Post the host's name near your monitor and use it regularly during the interview.*

- ❖ *If you make the host look good, it will actually pay off for you in the long run!*

- ❖ *Add value to the podcast with a free offer. It will help drive traffic to your own site.*

- ❖ *Ensure that you have a strong call to action and that you are asking for exactly what you want.*

- ❖ *Follow up with a card and/or small thank-you gift for the host. Remember: Podcast marketing is all about building relationships.*

CHAPTER FOUR:
GETTING A RETURN ON YOUR INVESTMENT

At this point, you understand the critical importance of sound quality for both the audience and the host, you have a quality microphone and the right place in which to record, your website and one sheet are ready to go, comments on social media are positive and helpful, you've positioned yourself as a celebrity and know what valuable things you have to say and have practiced, practiced, practiced. You also have a checklist list of follow-up steps to take after the interview is over.

Great. Good job. But the big question remains: "Once I do all of these things, how do I get a return on my investment?"

Excellent question. Of course you want a return on your investment or why else would you be taking the necessary steps to be a guest expert on podcasts?

Remember what I told you at the beginning of the book about using podcasting as part of your overall marketing strategy? This marketing component – and it is only *one* of the pieces of your entire marketing effort – is not a quick fix for a struggling business. You will not see results five minutes after the podcast goes live on iTunes. As with building celebrity, it takes some time and it takes some patience, and with those, it will pay off. But the time it takes is certainly shortened compared to decades ago… in the pre-internet era!

Podcasting is marketing that is based on relationship building, both the relationships you build with podcast hosts as well as their listeners. The return on your investment comes from how you continue to leverage the relationships you create as a guest expert by delivering value to the show, making the host look good, and offering a giveaway to the audience that will drive them to your site to begin solidifying the relationship that started when they listened to what you had to say and share on the podcast. There is a "know, like, and trust" sequence that has to occur before prospects will buy from you. By being a guest expert on a podcast, you will certainly get the audience to know you. Heck, they may even like you by the end of the show. Gaining trust takes more time.

*"Every sale has five basic obstacles: no need, no money, no hurry, no desire, **no trust.**"*

~ Zig Ziglar

Yes, gaining trust takes time, but it is a critical component of your success as an entrepreneur. That's why I keep reiterating the importance of building relationships with your prospects in your marketing efforts, especially podcasting.

Picking the Right Podcasts

With the exploding popularity of podcasts in recent years, there are thousands of interview-based podcasts on iTunes. When you are working to grow your business as a guest expert, it can be difficult to know which shows you should be on. Contrary to popular belief, "big" shows with huge download numbers are not necessarily the answer.

Before you start sending mass pitch emails to every podcast you can find, consider these criteria to determine if the podcast is a good fit for you. The first part of getting a return on your investment is to be sure the podcast makes sense for your business.

First, the podcast should speak to your target audience. Who is your ideal customer? Hopefully you already know that answer and have a clear vision about your ideal customer, including their demographics, backgrounds, perhaps location, spending habits, pain points, etc. Figure out what sorts of podcasts your target audience listens to. You can easily reverse engineer it by knowing the pain points of your target audience and determining which shows provide solutions to those pain points. Those are the podcasts your target audience is very likely listening to.

It doesn't matter whether the show has a huge audience or a small one. What matters is that you are reaching your target market. Which is better? Being on a podcast with a huge audience in which only a tiny fraction are interested in what you have to say (or sell) or having a small audience with almost every single listener engaged in what you're offering? I'll go with an engaged audience every time.

Second, make sure the podcast resonates with your own message. In order to deliver interviews that will generate leads, you need to be on podcasts in which your message will resonate. If you are a holistic medicine expert, your message will most likely fall on deaf ears if you are interviewed on a real estate podcast. That doesn't mean, however, you need to *only* be on holistic medicine podcasts. Look for crossover and applicability. To be clichéd, think outside the box. For example, an interview on an entrepreneurial podcast may yield fantastic results, as holistic health and work/life balance is often a topic to which entrepreneurs relate. It's often a pain point for them and an issue with which they struggle.

Third, you want to be a guest expert on podcasts that have an engaged following. You will certainly be doing your part to get the word out about your appearance, so focus on podcasts that are also speaking to an engaged following. Does the podcast have a Facebook group with conversations happening between the host and the listeners? Does the podcast have a unique hashtag that unites the listeners and makes them feel like they're a part of a community? Shows with an engaged following are more likely to connect with the guests. When that connection exists, you are better positioned to leverage it to boost your own return on investment.

Finally, podcasts that have show notes with links can grease the skids for post-show access. While show notes are certainly not a requirement for a great podcast, look for show notes on the podcast's website. These make the awesome content you deliver more accessible for listeners, and since most listeners will hear your interview while on-the-go, a great show notes page will give them a reliable place to find your contact information as well as links to your website.

Don't make the mistake of equating a podcast with huge numbers of downloads as the right choice. You want your message to resonate, and it's better to have a smaller but **engaged** *audience!*

Marketing Puzzle Pieces

Podcasting is only one of several pieces of the marketing puzzle, and it takes time before the right people hear your show, join your community, opt in to your email list, and get to know, like, and trust you enough before they invest financially in your products and services… before they open their wallets and hand you money.

In order to truly get a return on investment from podcasting, you must build out a full marketing platform. You already know that your site has to be in tiptop shape, but there's more to a profitable marketing platform than a website. At his Dream Business Academy live events, Dream Business Coach, Jim Palmer teaches what a million-dollar marketing platform looks like. Here's the snapshot of what it includes:

- Video marketing
- Podcasting

- Speaking and interviews
- Social media marketing
- Becoming an author
- Content marketing

In order to truly get a return on your investment as a guest expert on a podcast, you must have the whole marketing platform in place, so people who hear you on a podcast have more of your content to consume when they land on your website.

Personally, I have the perfect example of why that's true: When I was at Social Media Marketing World 2015 in San Diego, a man named Adrion Porter approached me on the first day of the conference and introduced himself. He told me he'd listened to my interview on *Leaders in the Trenches*, hosted by Gene Hammett. He went on to download my podcast, *Rhodes to Success*. After enjoying my podcast, he found my web TV show, *Interview Connections TV*. After that, he invited several of our Interview Connections guest expert clients on his podcast and has also been a guest on my show. The relationship that has evolved has paid off for both of us.

Now, imagine if he heard my interview on *Leaders in the Trenches*, went to my website, and found a sales page with no free, valuable content to consume! We never would have met at the conference because he would not have known what I looked like (hint, hint... do videos!) and all the amazing interviews we connected him with would not have happened. If you want to check out my interview with Adrion on *Rhodes to Success*, visit http://www.jessicarhodes.biz/adrion/ and a full transcript of it is included in the Resource section at the end of this book.

Videos

Video marketing is by far my favorite kind of marketing. Not only does it allow people to hear your voice, but it also shows your audience what you look like, how you speak, facial expressions, body language, etc. Videos can be a scary medium to take on because it is entirely transparent, and we often feel that if the videos aren't perfect, they're not worth publishing. Hear this: You are your own worst critic! Some of my most viewed videos are the ones with no makeup, wearing jeans and a t-shirt! People love to see the real you. You're more relatable that way!

Here are some action steps for you to get started in video marketing:

1. Write a list of the ten most frequently asked questions that you get from your clients or that are typical in your industry.
2. Set up your camera (iPhone is fine!) on a tripod or use a selfie stick while walking!
3. Film 10 two-minute videos answering each question.
4. Schedule them to release weekly on Facebook and on YouTube and embed the videos from YouTube onto your blog.

That is it! That's all there is. In time, I'd recommend coming up with a name for your "web TV show," but to start, simply film several videos and get them online. Are you thinking, "Podcast interviews are enough for me, Jessica!"? Well, that's fine. But remember, if you want to see a return on your investment, then you need more content for podcast listeners to consume once they get to your website, and short, content-rich videos are an excellent way to engage new fans and followers.

Blogs

People consume content in different ways, depending on their own preferences. Some people prefer to listen, others like to watch videos, and some people prefer to read. I like to read, listen, *and* watch videos, but it depends on the type of content I'm consuming and when I get the content that determines which format makes the most sense for me. If I'm browsing the web while watching TV, I'm not going to watch a video or listen to a podcast, but I will gladly read a blog post. There are also a lot of people who don't have the patience to listen to a whole podcast, and they can consume the content quicker if they are reading, so videos are not ideal in this case either. For these reasons, I advise that you transcribe your videos and podcasts, as well as write a blog.

To get your blog going, follow the same action steps from my section about video marketing. Instead of filming 10 two-minute videos, simply write out your answers to the questions you are most frequently asked... or the questions that are most frequent in your industry or profession. If you haven't been asked a lot of questions yet, go into the Facebook groups and LinkedIn forums where your target audience is hanging out and take note of the most frequently asked questions from group members. If writing is really a struggle for you, there are literally hundreds of ghostwriters and virtual assistants who can help.

Podcasts

Lastly, if you want to see a return on your investment as a guest expert on podcasts, hosting your own podcast is a huge step! Here are some of the top reasons that you'd want to host your own podcast:

1. When you interview people on your show who had you on theirs, you will deepen your relationship with them.
2. You get big brownie points with podcasters who interview you. It gives you credibility and demonstrates that you're simply ***not*** trying to profit off of someone else's audience that they worked so hard to build.
3. As a guest on other podcasts, the people who are discovering you already like listening to podcasts, so they

are much more likely to want to listen to your show, as opposed to reading a blog or watching videos.

Without a doubt, producing your own podcast is a lot more work than writing a blog or filming videos and uploading them to Facebook and YouTube. However, the bigger the investment, the bigger the return! I've dedicated the second half of this book to hosting your own show, so keep reading!

Promoting Your Interview

In order to leverage your appearance on a podcast as a guest expert, you have to help promote it. Don't rely solely on how the host promotes the show. More importantly, the host will certainly appreciate expanding the audience to include your own customers, prospects, and followers. Think of that as another block or brick in the relationship you are building.

You have to promote your interview. Don't rely on the host to handle all of the promotion, or you are missing huge opportunities for return on your investment!

Social media is certainly an excellent tool for podcast promotion. Social media thrives on content. I create a lot of content. I'm frequently interviewed on other podcasts; I host my own podcast and co-host another; I create a weekly video and blog, and send an email and print newsletter. Without a proper social media strategy, I would not have nearly as many eyes and ears on my content as I currently enjoy.

While I believe that it's important to build your marketing platform on your own website – a place that you own and control – social media sites (Facebook, Twitter, LinkedIn, etc.) do have a place in your marketing strategy. Social media is most likely the

Interview Connections

top referral source from which you'll get prospects to your site, so do not neglect it.

With the expansion of social media sites, you can spend a lot of time with this marketing effort. I suggest you determine the top two or three social media platforms where your target audience is spending their time. You don't want to spend hours and hours building your LinkedIn presence if your target audience is over on Facebook or vice versa. As with all successful marketing, you have to direct your efforts toward where your prospects are most likely to see them.

When you've determined which social media platforms are best suited for you, implement a strategy that will establish you as an authority figure to your followers on those sites. When I started seriously investing in my social marketing strategy, I'll admit that I was a little hesitant at first because I wasn't sure it was worth it. However, after a few months of "being everywhere," I started to see real results. More podcast hosts were requesting me on their shows and comments started rolling in: "Jessica is really making a splash in podcasting." And, "Everyone knows you and is talking about you!"

When your content begins dominating social media, it shows that you are extraordinarily relevant and that you have important information to share. When it seems like you have a lot of important, relevant information, people will listen. Better still, people will seek you out.

Here are three simple tips to using social media to promote your podcast interviews:

1. **Consistently post your interviews.** When you know your episode is live, post a link on your social media, so your followers can hear the interview. You can't rely on the host to do all of the promoting because they may not be promoting to *your* audience. Take the initiative and share your interviews with your social network.

2. Give people a reason to listen to the interview. Don't simply post the link and leave it at that. Write a quick blurb to go with it that entices people to click the link and listen. Share a great quote, memorable moment, or even create your own awesome promotional graphic to drive people to the interview. Pique their interest to click!

3. Maximize engagements. No matter which social media platform you are using, make sure to tag the host and any business/podcast pages. By doing so, you are notifying the host and their network of your interview to get the greatest reach and traction. If a host posts the episode themselves (and hopefully tags you), respond with a like, comment, share, etc. Show your appreciation for being on the show and share the love! And don't forget to do the same when listeners are commenting on the interviews as well. Join that conversation with additional relevant, beneficial information.

Along these same lines, leave ratings and reviews for the shows that you listen to and love. Also, join and participate in Facebook and/or LinkedIn groups, Google circles, etc. With social media, it's all about participating in conversations. When you are part of the conversation, it helps position you as a go-to authority in your niche, gets your name and expertise in front of hosts who would be interested in interviewing your for their podcasts, and allows you to leverage interviews you've already done by referring people to those.

In a nutshell: create a ton of content in different formats, promote it on social media and to your list, and you will see your following and business grow.

Getting Publicity

Getting publicity is certainly a way to also get a return on your investment as a guest expert on podcasts. It can help jump start your promotion and get your message out. However, there are four very important things to keep in mind.

First, podcast interviews are not like "traditional" media interviews. There are a lot of differences, but the biggest one has to do with timing. Traditional media exposure tends to be live and as such, topical. Podcast interviews, on the other hand, present evergreen content, so they do not become dated. Podcasts are on-demand content – consumers can listen when and where they want. I consistently get leads from interviews I did years ago, not simply from the recent ones. If a listener hears dated information, they're very, very likely to tune out and turn off.

Second, podcasting is a long-term marketing strategy as I've reiterated many times. Getting booked on ten shows then stopping your podcast "tour" is not an effective way to grow your business as a guest expert. Like any marketing strategy, you need to commit for the long term to see results. Also, keep in mind that just because you record an interview now doesn't mean it will be published immediately. It may not be published for several weeks or months. Most podcasters batch produce their shows, handling post-production tasks later and then scheduling the podcast for release.

Since we're talking about podcast release timing, I want to take a minute to discuss using podcasts to launch a book. I'm often contacted by book launch managers or publicists who tell me, "My client is launching a book next month, and we need to get him 12 interviews on podcasts to launch it." If you're a podcaster, you know what my reaction to this is. This is horrible timing. Whether you're an author or publicist and want to use podcast interviews to launch a book, you need to plan ahead, and by ahead, I mean months and months in advance.

Getting a Return on Your Investment

What the author or publicist needs in the example I just shared are interview shows, effectively traditional media. Podcasts are **on-demand** interview shows, and they are not the same. My tip is to start at least six months in advance if you really want to use podcast interview shows for your book tour, and I hate to call it that because podcasts are about relationship building, not promotion.

Podcasts as relationship builders is the third thing to keep in mind when you or your publicist is thinking of using podcast interview shows as a marketing strategy. They're about networking and provide a way for both the host and the audience to connect with you. When you give a great interview and really connect with the host, you're welcomed into their network where you're introduced to a lot of new leads. Word of mouth is big in the podcasting world, so take the time to make meaningful connections and watch your reach grow exponentially.

Finally, as a reminder: Focus on niche shows, not just the big ones. If you only focus on shows with huge download numbers, you are going to miss the listeners that you want to and need to reach. If you really want a return on your investment, it is critically important to focus on podcasts that are speaking directly to your target audience. Focus on the shows that reach those specific people, no matter how small or large that podcast might be.

We've covered all the nuts and bolts you need to become and excel as a guest expert on podcasts to market your business. As I said in the beginning and will reiterate now, podcasting as a marketing tool is not a quick fix. It takes effort, time, and patience, but it will pay off! Every relationship you create and build will continue to provide you with other opportunities to market and grow your business.

At this point, perhaps you're ready to jump in as a guest expert on podcasts. If you have all the pieces in place that I've covered so far, I say, "Go for it!" I encourage you to check out InterviewConnections.com to discover how my team and I can expedite the effort and start booking you on the podcasts that make the most sense for you and your business.

Establishing yourself as a guest expert is a great way to start using podcasting as part of your marketing strategy. The startup costs are minimal (headshot, one sheet, microphone), and you can learn what it's like to speak behind a microphone and learn the ropes from an experienced podcast host. You also have the opportunity to build an audience before you launch your own show. Finally, you can perfect your content as a guest expert that will help you hone your focus for your own podcast if you choose to head down that road.

On the other hand, perhaps you find podcasting very intriguing and want to learn more about hosting your own show… right now. If that's the case, I say, "Read on!"

#ROCKTHEPODCAST Recap:

- *Podcasting as a marketing tool is a long-term commitment. If you expect to see sales flowing in five minutes after your interview goes live on iTunes, you will be disappointed.*

- *Being a guest expert on a podcast is the perfect way to build the "know, like, and trust" factor with the audience.*

- *Pick the right podcasts. Shows with large download numbers aren't necessarily the right ones. You want the podcast to speak to your target audience and for your message to resonate with them.*

- *Picking a podcast with an engaged following and one that publishes show notes can grease the skids for your return on investment.*

- *Podcasting is one piece of a content marketing program that should also include videos, blogs, and other content formats.*

- *You have to promote the podcast! Don't rely solely on the host to handle promotion or you will dramatically limit your ability to get a return on your investment. The host will also appreciate you promoting it to your audience and followers!*

- *Social media, when used correctly, provides a great avenue for promoting your interviews.*

- *Don't forget to join the conversation in social media groups and sites and to leave comments and reviews.*

PART 2:
ROCK THE PODCAST AS A HOST

CHAPTER FIVE:
HOW TO LAUNCH AND THEN SOAR

You're an expert in your niche and you've been sharing your valuable insight as a guest expert on podcasts. You understand that this platform makes sense in your marketing toolbox. You're building relationships through the interviews in which you've participated. Perhaps you are now at the point at which you see real value in hosting your own podcast. To that I say, "Go for it… but keep reading first!" We're about to delve into what happens on the other side of the microphone.

I understand that the decision to launch your own show is a big one and can feel quite daunting. It was for me. In August 2014 while flying home from the inaugural Podcast Movement conference, I decided to launch my podcast. But it was a decision that was not without some fear and trepidation. With a growing business in which I was aggressively investing and a toddler at home, it was a big pill to swallow. I had no idea how to edit a show in GarageBand, the music creation studio software that I use. (To be completely honest, I still struggle with that.) I wasn't sure what to say in my intro or what kind of music to use and the technical side looked like a huge learning curve.

The whole venture seemed overwhelming, so I worked through it with my business coach and figured it out, putting pieces in place one at a time. Once I had all those pieces in place, the podcast became another aspect of my business that I enjoy and no longer find overwhelming. It is an aspect of my marketing strategy that is providing a return on investment now and has helped me really grow my business.

If you're in the same boat that I was in 2014, let me assure you that the information I'm about to share will help you get past that sense of being overwhelmed. Even if you aren't certain that hosting your own show is the right choice for you, I encourage you to keep reading. Invest another couple hours with this book to get a sense of how hosting a show works. By the end, you may realize that it is for you!

Podcast Launch Blueprint

Having worked through the pieces of my own podcast with my business coach, I'd like to share my podcast launch blueprint that I've refined having launched two of my own successful podcasts and also having booked hundreds of guests for pre-launch shows in my business, Interview Connections.

Before I jump into the blueprint steps, let me first tell you that you must start with the end in mind. You have to know what your goal is for the podcast and be crystal clear about it. Where do you want your podcast to go? Is it only to market your business or perhaps you envision it becoming its own revenue-generating entity? You have to know what your goal is before you begin investing time and money into your effort or you will never get the results you want!

Commit: The biggest pitfall I see new podcasters fall victim to is a fear of commitment. They are afraid to commit to a launch date for their show. I firmly believe that you should set a launch date, carve it in stone, and stick to it! Without a launch date, you will get stuck in the mode of planning: plan and plan and plan without actually starting!

Set a date on which you will actively launch and promote your show. (The exact day the show is live on iTunes may be different from the launch date because once you submit the show to iTunes, it may take a few days to a couple weeks for it to be live.) About 60 days is a good time frame from idea to launch. It allows enough time for you to plan but not so much time that it never becomes a priority for you and continually is moved down your to-do list. Set a date. Stick to it.

Perfection Kills: Your podcast will not be that good when you launch. Just accept that. I can't even bring myself to listen to my first few episodes because I'm pretty sure I would embarrass myself. It takes time for every new podcaster to find their groove! Do not focus on launching a perfect podcast... or you never will! I can't remember who said it, but I quote, "If you aren't embarrassed by your first few episodes, you waited too long to launch."

Additionally, as soon as you explore various Facebook groups and online forums for podcasters, you will be quickly overwhelmed by all the marketing tactics and launch strategies that you'll find there. There are countless marketers teaching new podcasters how to game the iTunes system to get to the top of New and Noteworthy. Friend, ignore them all... or at least most of them! You never win with an attempt to game the system. Successful podcasters are not those who are number one in New and Noteworthy. Successful podcasters are those who stick with it and keep publishing, consistently delivering valuable content to their listeners.

You can also quickly bog down in the technical side of podcasting: how to record, getting a mixer, audio editing software, etc. as well as artwork and audio branding. It can range from a simple Skype recording to a $1,500 set up. While I wanted my own podcast to be as professional as possible, I also knew that if I got too wrapped up in the complexities, I would not make my pre-determined October 1st launch date. The old "analysis paralysis" in full swing!

A perfect podcast on your desktop is not as good as an imperfect one already on iTunes with people listening to it.

As with anything in business, it's more important to implement and take massive action if you want to be successful. Getting stuck in pre-launch activities won't help you. Yes, you need pre-launch planning but sticking to your date is more important. Your podcast isn't doing anyone any good if it's sitting on your computer without anyone to listen to it. You can and will improve as you go. Move at the speed of instruction. Do the best you can with what you have.

Focusing a ton of your energy on launch and your iTunes ranking will burn you out. Podcasting is long term – a marathon, not a sprint. If you put most of your resources (your time and money) on the launch, you will quickly lose sight of the long-term vision for your show. It's like getting married: If all of your focus is on the wedding rather than the marriage that follows it, you are going to struggle in the weeks, months, and years that follow. Likewise, if you're expecting and all you do is read about childbirth but not parenting, you're doing yourself and your child a huge disservice. The wedding and birth are only the start. The real game is the marriage and child-rearing. The launch is only the start. The real game is ongoing shows that offer value to listeners.

So if the launch and your iTunes ranking aren't worth focusing on, what is? The answer is simple: really great content. Dave Jackson, host of *The School of Podcasting* speaks about the importance of creating compelling content. While I've stressed sound quality earlier in the book, I assure you, it comes in behind quality content. Don't stress about whether you should get the ATR2100 or Blue Yeti microphone as most listeners won't know the difference. Yes, a quality microphone is important but your content is even more so!

Production Basics: Podcasting may feel like a daunting task, even when you are on board with my "just focus on compelling content" mantra. I produce my weekly podcast in about two hours a month. Follow these steps, and you can, too.

- Use Skype to connect with guests and Ecamm call recorder to record. If you have a PC, Pamela is the best call recorder to use.
- I recommend using the ATR 2100. It's not very expensive and has great sound quality.

- As far as editing goes, if you're determined to do-it-yourself, you can use GarageBand or Audacity. But quite frankly, if you don't already know how to edit audio, spend your time on high revenue-generating activities in your business and outsource this task. I use Podfly Productions. They're amazing!
- Libsyn.com is what I use to host my podcast online; they offer great stats, and their platform is pretty easy to figure out.
- I worked with a graphic designer to design my artwork. Her name is Caye Howe and her website is FireFlyGraphics.com
- I do not upload my podcast myself; Podfly does that for me. I record my show, put it in Dropbox, and the guys at Podfly upload it to Libsyn and to my website for me.
- I had the voiceover work for my intro done by someone on Fiverr.com, and the music is my brother's band, The Danger O's. Do you have any musician friends? I recommend asking them for your podcast music! It sounds far better than the stock music that you'll find online, and they'll likely get some new fans out of it; just link to them in your show notes.
- I also use a virtual assistant to write my show notes and another virtual assistant create the graphics for each episode.

Following those steps enables me to get my podcast completed in about two hours each month. As you can see, I outsource* quite a bit of the technical parts. It's an investment of about $400 to $500, and I find it to be worth every penny. If I tried to tackle all of the technical aspects of show production, it would cost far, far more than that in terms of the value of my time. By outsourcing these tasks, I can focus on running and growing

Interview Connections, and I have the time I need for revenue-producing activities.

*For complete transparency, I am not an affiliate of any of the mentioned products or providers. I recommend them because I know they do great work and that you will also likely get a ton of great value by working with them as well.

Longevity

It is difficult to keep podcasting after three to six months when you're not seeing a financial return on your investment and no one from your audience is engaging with you. The reality is that it can take a long time to see a return on your podcasting investment. Marketing is long term, and podcasting is not direct response marketing. You don't podcast to get people to sign up with your products and services right away. You podcast both as a guest expert and a host to build a relationship with your following. I have been podcasting for a couple of years, and people are just starting to really take action.

Recently I had a client sign up. I had not had a conversation with her, but she opted for a six-month package with us. When I talked to her, I realized that she had been listening to my podcasts and consuming all of my content. She had been listening to me on my shows, *The Podcast Producers* and *Rhodes to Success* and other shows, and I had no idea that she was a listener until she actually signed up.

Remember this: Buyers buy when they're ready to buy, so if you aren't hearing from your listeners, don't abandon your effort because it takes time. People need to get to know you. They need to really experience your content for a long time before they take action. Don't stop. Don't give up. Stick with it because people are out there listening to you, reading your blog, watching your videos, and when they are ready, they will sign up.

So, what can help you increase your podcasting longevity? How do you make it to 50 episodes or 100 episodes? How do you get to a year and keep the show going?

You have to love it.

I will be the first to admit that I do not love everything I do in my business. I love my business, but there are always tasks that are not as enjoyable as others, and I am not afraid to admit that. Heck, writing this book has been at the bottom of my priority list because of all the things I do to market my business, writing does not come naturally to me. However, just because I don't love writing, doesn't mean I don't still do it. It doesn't mean I don't have a blog and I don't publish e-books. I find ways to get the writing done by leveraging the talents of people around me. For example, my Director of Marketing, Angela Greaser, now writes my blog for me by repurposing the content I've been creating for years on my podcasts and in my videos. It's my voice and my expertise, but I have someone else put their fingers on the keyboard.

Some podcasters believe they have to have an avatar: an image of their perfect listener and direct the show to that person. For me to continue my love of podcasting, I'm the one who has to be interested in the show. Perhaps I am my own avatar. Regardless, if you aren't interested in your own show, no one else will be... even if they might be the perfect listener.

Chances are excellent that people are listening to you but they aren't quite ready to buy yet. Stick with it!

If you love podcasting, you won't have trouble keeping your show going for a long time. Most people quit their show because it either falls too low on their priority list, or they just don't love doing it. If there are aspects of podcasting that you don't love, outsource those.

To keep the show high on your priority list, let's have a little "Mr. T. in-your-face" talk here.

Make it a priority. Look around at all the successful entrepreneurs and marketers who have big followings and are interviewed all the time on podcasts. Most of them are marketing their businesses by podcasting, blogging, doing videos, writing books, speaking, and going to conferences. In short, they are hustling and doing the hard work it takes to grow a successful business. They know that not every marketing tactic will result in a lot of direct sales, but like ingredients in a soup, it's all necessary for the best outcome. My coach, Jim Palmer, shares a powerful comment to our mastermind group. Before he started hosting live events to grow his coaching business, a mentor asked him, "What makes you think you deserve the same level of success as other people when *you're not willing to do the work* they're doing?"

You cannot expect to grow a big following and increase your business's revenue and net profits if you are not willing to invest in your business! Podcasting is an investment, and I know it produces a huge return when implemented correctly. Interview Connections books thousands of interviews each year, and we have countless stories of entrepreneurs getting new clients from their podcasts. It's worth the time, so don't put it at the bottom of your priority list!

Rekindle your love for podcasting. A lot of podcasters know they *should* be podcasting, but the reason they quit their show is because they just don't love doing it. It sucks their energy and becomes a grind. Corey Coates and I produced an amazing 10-episode audio series about the art and business of podcasting in Season 1 of *The Podcast Producers*. It was a ton of work, but we absolutely loved it, so putting in the work was not a drag. Then it came time to plan for Season 2. We love podcasting together and we love our audience, but doing another highly produced and edited audio series felt like a grind that neither of us was that interested in pursuing it again. However, we didn't want to quit the show. We had raving fans who kept saying they could not wait for Season 2. We didn't want to stop podcasting together. So what did we do?

We changed the whole format of the show. With a few clear goals in mind, we came up with a new format that made the show an enjoyable venture for us both. The big obstacle to us enjoying the show going into Season 2 was that we felt like we had all these people to please. We felt like we had all these expectations from listeners that we had to meet and that, in and of itself, became a burden. By only focusing on what we wanted in the show, it opened up all these new possibilities.

If you are finding that your show isn't enjoyable anymore, consider changing the format, the schedule by which you release episodes, or the topics you focus on.

If your show feels like a grind, it's almost impossible to keep that from coming across to your audience.

Corey and I knew the show would feel like a grind if we had a weekly release schedule. Doing one episode every week was going to be too much to sustain considering how busy we both are in our businesses. So, we decided to only produce two podcast episodes a month.

In my podcast, *Rhodes to Success*, I realized that not only do I enjoy interviewing fellow podcasters about podcasting, but my audience likes those episodes more, too! So, I decided to not focus on broader business and marketing topics and gear the show more toward podcasting topics. This helps me enjoy the podcast more and attracts more listeners to me.

Michael Hyatt, host of *This Is Your Life*, made a big change after producing 100 episodes. He hired a co-host who would come on to the show and interview him each and every episode. This took away all his prep work and made the show something he loved again.

To rekindle your love for podcasting, don't feel like you need to do a giant re-branding or relaunch of your podcast every time you change it up. Just make the changes necessary to keep going... and keep going... and keep going. Longevity garners positive results.

Quality First

If you follow me on social media, read my blog or watch my videos, you've heard me talk about why download stats for your podcast don't matter. But I'm going to take a few minutes to cover when and why they may be important.

To start, I need to be clear that the actual **number** of download numbers per episode don't matter to me. What I analyze are the trends in my stats; when downloads decline, when they stay the same, when they increase... and why. When I see that little orange line go up, it means my audience is growing. That tells me that I'm honing in on my target market and delivering content that they find valuable. It tells me that putting quality first is paying off. It also tells me I'm reaching more people as my business and my podcast grow.

Growing an audience takes time. It took a solid year of producing and fine-tuning my podcast before I saw my audience increase. By staying connected with my audience, I have been able to make adjustments to my show and establish myself as an expert in my niche.

While ramping up my marketing strategy has helped grow my audience and connect with my listeners, remember that great marketing can't make up for a bad podcast. You can't polish a turd! Don't get so focused on "growing your audience" that the quality of your show falls by the wayside. I did not invest in much marketing for my podcast until a year after I launched. Today, I invest in a social media manager, and I recently invested in Meet Edgar to repost my old content as well. Have these marketing strategies helped grow my podcast? The answer is an unequivocal

YES! But don't forget, the quality of your show is most important. In addition to ramping up my marketing, I also have improved the quality of my production and my interview skills. I have continued to improve as I went rather than trying to be perfect from the start.

If you host your podcast on Libsyn or another hosting service, you can easily log in to check your own download numbers and trend data. Keep in mind as you review your data that it is *not* the number of downloads that matters. What truly matters are the people behind those numbers. Even if you aren't seeing growth or maybe you are even seeing a decline, take a step back and evaluate how you are engaging with your listeners. If your stats are doing down but your engagements are going up, you are on the right track! You are homing in on your target market and reaching the people who are truly going to benefit from your show. And those are the people who are going to eventually convert into paying customers and grow your business.

Podcasting is so much more than stats and download numbers. Podcasting is connecting with real people.

Entertainment Value

You're an expert. You have valuable information to share with your audience. You can help them solve problems. All of that makes for great content; however, you also have to be entertaining. You're connecting with people. People want to be entertained. You don't have to be a stand-up comedian, but you do have to be at least a bit entertaining. It adds to the "know, *like*, and trust" factor that prospects have to have before they'll buy from you.

If you are looking for a unique way to engage your listeners *before* they hear even one of your episodes, try creating a video trailer for your podcast!

As I've mentioned, I co-host *The Podcast Producers* with my good friend, Corey Coates. We wanted to give our listeners, old and new, a taste of what they could expect in the upcoming season. The trailer we created for it gave viewers a clear picture of the show. Not only did we share what the show is and what topics we would cover, we also introduced the hosts, the guests, the launch date, the website, and more all in 90 seconds.

Video trailers deliver so much more than just information – they bring visual perspective to an audio medium. Trailers help listeners put a face to the voice they hear, building instant rapport. *The Podcast Producers'* trailer not only gives you a "behind-the-scenes" look at the hosts, it gives you a personal look at the guests as well. With videos like this, you're starting to build connections and establish familiarity before an episode even airs. You're being entertaining.

So whether you are starting a new podcast, launching a new season, or even right in the middle of your normal episode releases, consider developing a trailer for your show. You'll be able to connect with your audience – and attract new listeners as well!

#ROCKTHEPODCAST Recap:

- *If you decide to host your own podcast, pick a launch date and stick to it. Yes, allow yourself planning time (60 days works), and launch on your selected date. You will never be successful when you are stuck in analysis paralysis.*

- *Perfection kills. Accept your first shows will not be perfect. Get them launched and improve as you go!*

- *Focus on content! You will never game the ranking system. In the end, quality content always wins.*

- *Outsourcing the technical side of your podcast can pay off. Your time is better spent focusing on the show and your own core competencies in your business.*

- *Podcasting is long-term marketing. You have to stick with it to see results. To stick with it, you also have to love it!*

- *If you lose your love of podcasting, you'll have to rekindle it. If you don't love your show, your audience definitely won't. Reformat or change it up as you need to.*

- *Quality first! I only use stats to watch trends. If your download numbers decline but your engagement goes up, you are on the right track!*

- *Be entertaining.*

How to Launch and Then Soar

CHAPTER SIX:
LEVERAGING THE POWER OF GUEST INTERVIEWS

There are many different podcast formats you can adopt for your show. You can have a solo podcast in which it's just you talking. You can co-host a show, have a roundtable discussion podcast, or you can interview guests. The choice is yours and depends on what you want your podcast to achieve in terms of your marketing.

As the founder of Interview Connections, the premier source for booking outstanding podcast guests, I love interview-based podcasts. We book our guest expert clients for interviews on shows in their target markets, and we help our podcaster clients find and book guests on their own shows. In booking thousands of interviews a year, our team constantly hears stories of how podcasters and guests grow their businesses by leveraging the relationships they form doing interviews. So yes, I'm partial to the interview format for podcasting because I've seen firsthand how wildly successful it has been for hundreds of my clients.

Let's jump into this chapter in which I will teach you how to find and book guests, how to work with guests, hone your interview skills, the pros and cons of interviewing celebrities, and the best kinds of guests you should interview in order to leverage your podcast to truly grow your business.

There are three main benefits of interviewing guests for your podcast. First, it helps you produce a lot more content for your audience and deliver more value to your listeners than you could alone. When you host a solo show, or even a co-hosted podcast, you have to develop **all the content**. On the other hand, when you interview guests, those interviews naturally produce the content. Interviewing guests on your show also helps position you to your audience as a well-connected entrepreneur.

When you deliver a new guest every week, your listeners start to take note. Also, when you are bringing guests to your audience that they've never heard of before ("no names") but are amazing guests with valuable content, your listeners will be eager to hear who you introduce them to next! Lastly, interviewing guests on your podcast helps you build valuable and profitable relationships that lead to future business profits.

Using Social Media to Find Guests

A great place to find guests for your podcast is on social media. My favorite platform and the site with which I have had the most success is Twitter. Twitter is, ironically, the last social media platform that I joined, but it is now my favorite, for business anyway. The key feature I want you to focus on in Twitter is following. When you follow someone, Twitter loads three similar users for you to also consider following. This has been incredibly helpful in allowing me to find guests for Interview Connections clients' podcasts because it introduces me to people I never would have found otherwise. The platform's built-in, behind-the-scenes algorithms are doing the hard work and heavy lifting of making viable connections.

Twitter is also the easiest platform to connect directly with the actual person rather than their assistant or staff. On Facebook, it's harder to connect with the actual person because you first have to friend them, they have to accept you, and then you message them. Or if they don't accept your friend request, you have to like their business page and write on their wall or message the page, and these wall posts and messages are often overlooked. I also find that entrepreneurs are outsourcing their social media management on their business Facebook pages more than other platforms.

With Twitter, you can tweet someone without them having to follow you, so it makes it very easy to initiate a conversation regarding an interview on your podcast. I recommend not giving away too many details about your request in this initial tweet. I usually tweet something like, "Hi @guest! Can we connect about an interview request?" It is very effective to contact them initially over Twitter because emails are often overlooked or even deleted if they are sent by an unknown contact. If you do email the guest first, you can send them a tweet that reads, "Hi @guest! Just wanted to let you know I emailed you with an interview request!" By doing this, you are helping to draw their attention to your email.

I assure you, "interview request" is a very powerful phrase! It's an attention grabber and immediately gives the recipient a sense of importance: "Wow, someone wants to interview me. I have to respond to this to learn more." Honestly, it's an ego stroke, and it's human nature to feel good about that.

Pinterest is another site on which you can find great guests. Pinterest is unique because it acts as a search engine. If you're looking for guests who are marketing experts, you can search Pinterest for "podcast interview marketing expert" and get different results than what you'd receive from Google or other search engines because, unlike a search engine that is searching the entire web, Pinterest is showing only the results that individual users have chosen to pin to their boards.

Other Resources to Find Guests

Amazon is very powerful tool to find great guests because it gives you a huge library of authors from which to choose. Decide the topic you want to cover in your podcast and search for books on that topic. When you find a book that *fits your topic well*, click through and find the author. Many authors will have an Amazon author page on which you can discover their biography and contact information. Some author profiles even link to their Twitter profiles.

I recommend also filtering your results by publication date and research the authors who have released a book recently. Authors are almost always willing to do interviews when they have recently released a book because they want to get as much media exposure for it as possible.

When you reach out to an author to be a guest on your show, be sure to position your podcast as credible, established, and with an audience. This is where using a virtual assistant or Interview Connections to book guests comes in handy because authors often have a public relations representative or a publishing agency schedule their interviews, and these individuals really make sure they qualify which interview opportunities will be worthwhile for their clients. When you have representation booking your guests, your podcast looks like the real deal because it shows that you have invested in its success.

Authors often make great guests, and you'll find millions of them on Amazon. Research topics that make sense for your podcast and reach out to the author.

You can also use other podcasts to uncover guest experts that make sense for your show and who will resonate with your audience. Yes, your podcast is unique, but there are likely a lot of other podcasters who have interviewed the same types of guests that you also want to feature. Search through iTunes and listen to similar podcasts to find prospective guests. Reaching out to other podcasters for recommendations is very helpful because they can give you referrals of guests they've interviewed and know are great interviewees. Similarly, ask your guests for recommendations of people they know who would also be a great guest for your podcast.

Don't forget about using your personal network to find guests. Ask friends, colleagues, and peers who they might know who would be a good fit for your show and your audience.

Qualify Your Guests before Booking

It's inevitable that some interviewees will be duds. Not all guests are going to rock your socks off, but there are some things you can look for before booking your guests to determine whether or not they will be a great interviewee.

First, determine if they have ever been interviewed before on a podcast or radio show. By simply typing their name into iTunes, you will find other podcasts on which they have appeared. You can also search for their name on YouTube to see if they have been in any videos. If they have, listen to a podcast on which they were interviewed or watch them on a video, so you can assess their verbal communication skills and how they present themselves in general. Remember: As your guest, they are going to reflect a bit on your show. You want it to be good, or better still, great.

If you cannot find any interviews they have done or any videos they have produced but you found that they have great written content, set up a phone call with them to tell them more about the show and ask some initial questions before booking the interview. You can ask some of the same questions you would during the interview to not only learn more about them and how well their topic meshes with your show but also to hear how they answer questions and how they present themselves verbally.

As I said, your guest will reflect on your show, so if you find that they don't present well, that should be a red flag. In fairness, perhaps what you find and listen to is their first interview. If it seems their topic would really benefit your listeners, perhaps make note of them and check them out again in a few months to determine if they've done additional interviews and have improved their presentation.

One of the benefits of considering guest experts that have been interviewed for other podcasts is that you can get a referral from the podcast host about how the guest handled the interview and themselves (were they prompt in response, on time for the recording, did they have the needed technology, etc.), and you will obviously also have a chance to listen to the podcast yourself.

When it's time to book your guest, as I've mentioned, there are many benefits to using a virtual assistant or Interview Connections to handle this task for you. I actually launched this business because I saw a huge need for connecting great guests with podcast hosts. Our highly trained team of booking agents secures hundreds of interviews each month on industry specific podcasts. It's an expertise, like accounting or tax preparation, that makes a world of sense for you to outsource.

However, if you choose to book your own guests, I've included the transcription of a great interview I did with Adrion Porter, "How to Book Podcast Guests" in the Resource section at the end of this book. Whether or not you choose to book your own guests, that interview is definitely worth reading!

Working with Podcast Guests

If you want to have a successful, well-respected and highly recommended podcast, you need to make it super easy for your guests to be booked and scheduled! After all, if your guests enjoy their experience not only during the interview but before and after the recording, they'll become a raving fan and brand ambassador for your podcast.

First, make sure your "ask" is clear and specific, so your guest experts will have an understanding of what you want to talk to them about during the interview. A confused guest is a frustrated guest! Confusion is certainly no way to start the process.

Next, ensure the scheduling process also very, very easy. I recommend using scheduling software like Schedule Once. However, some guests will not want to use a software program and prefer a more personal touch. Never hesitate to call them and schedule a time manually.

Ask your guest for only what you *need*, not everything you *want*. Request the contact information you will need the day of the interview (Skype name and backup phone number), a brief bio or preferred introduction, headshot, and any preferred suggestions or talking points. Communicate the fact that you ask for talking points so that you can steer the conversation to focus on the topic that will best spotlight them!

If the guest doesn't schedule within two business days or they don't send the requested information, send a friendly reminder and follow up. Chances are they forgot!

Send a confirmation email before the recording with whatever additional information they may need to be prepared for during the interview (your questions, your Skype name, etc.), and most importantly, connect on social media and start building a relationship!

Now... while I've just suggested that you send talking points beforehand (and some guests may want to also receive actual questions instead), it really depends on your guest. When I interviewed David Ralph, financial trainer turned full-time podcaster, he likened an interview to a first date, suggesting that you wouldn't show up on a first date with a list of questions but rather engage each other back and forth in normal conversation. The more interesting podcasts can be the ones in which the audience isn't exactly sure what they're going to get. David prefers a "freestyle" approach rather than worrying about show flow.

A "freestyle" approach to the interview often creates greater interest and value for listeners. It's more conversational and creates stronger relationships.

In "freestyling," it's a natural conversation and creates deeper relationships. Conversations develop into relationships and relationships develop into business and business develops into sales.

Honing Your Interview Skills

When Podcast Movement 2015 took place in Texas, unfortunately I could not attend due to my pregnancy; however, I had an opportunity to watch some of the sessions online via Periscope. From the little bit I saw online, the biggest highlight and most important "take away" occurred when an attendee asked *WTF* podcast host, Marc Maron for his biggest tip for being a good interviewer. His answer was one word: "Listen."

Stephen Covey writes in *The 7 Habits of Highly Effective People* that you should seek first to understand, then to be understood. Think about it: When we are in a conversation with someone, most of the time our brains are thinking about what we want to say next. When you're thinking about what you're about to say (or ask), you cannot also be listening and fully absorbing and understanding what the other person is saying. So that one-word piece of advice – listen – speaks volumes!

Treat interviewing as an art and a craft. Anyone can turn on a mic and record a conversation; however, you have to put a lot of thought into your interviews. If you truly want to have a conversational interview (ala "freestyle"), you really have to listen.

When you have a guest on your podcast, make it your goal to get the guest talking about a topic that truly interests them, a topic about which they have a lot to say and one that lights them up.

(Side note: This is why I personally dislike scripted questions and interview shows with a set flow of questions. I believe questions need to be written for each guest personally, and podcasts are far better when they're personalized with the opportunity to follow the flow of the conversation.)

When you ask that first question and hear your guest start talking, don't look at your notes, don't think about what your next question will be, just listen very intently. Your next questions should help the guest dig deeper, clarify something they said, or build off of a story they shared.

Interviewing is more than asking questions. There may be times when you will need to take control of the conversation if your guest doesn't pause or wanders far from the topic at hand. It's a good idea to present a very lengthy introduction in which *you* tell the guest's keynote story which gives you an element of control. This is why it's important for you to have their bio in advance and do your homework and show preparation. Additionally, don't simply read the bio. Share your own impressions of your guest when you first learned about them and what they do. For example, "I was so impressed when I learned that they... fill in the blank." Provide your own backstory and personal reactions to your guest. Communicate why you are excited to be interviewing them.

Your guest introduction creates the whole vibe of the show. It can make or break it the listeners' interest in the show from the very start. Your guests will appreciate you building up the anticipation about what they are going to share rather than turning to them to handle their own introduction. Additionally, don't lead with the guest's name. It's a trick that every interviewer uses to keep listeners hooked. The last two words of your introduction should be the guest's name.

Keep in mind that not every episode is going to be a home run, and there have been times when I've debated whether or not to release a show. However, I do because there are usually at least a few nuggets for listeners. In fact, you may find that these shows are the ones that generate the most feedback from your audience. The "end product" is different for every single listener.

You should also be re-listening to your shows to determine how you can improve your interviewing skills. Yes, you'll be embarrassed by your first few shows – everyone is – but use your mistakes as education. By critiquing yourself, you will continue to gain confidence and make ongoing improvements. The better you become as a host and interviewer, the more relaxed your guests will be and that will add to the overall quality of your show. A great host can actually create a great guest.

In order to be a good interviewer, my last tip is to book guests that *you* are interested in speaking with. It's really hard to have chemistry with a guest who bores you, and when that's the case, your listeners will be disengaged too. The lack of excitement comes through loud and clear.

Celebrities or "No Names"

I have worked with podcasters at Interview Connections who only want to interview billionaires, celebrities, and people who have flown to the moon and back, and they expect to interview people like that before their show has launched and while their website is still under construction. What happens next is a harsh reality check! Just because you are starting a podcast does not mean you will land interviews with millionaires, billionaires, and household names, but that's not the worst thing.

There are pros and cons to interviewing big name celebrities in your industry. The biggest benefit to interviewing recognized celebrities on your podcast is that their name generates positive search results for you. If people are searching for the celebrity in a search engine or in the iTunes store, your podcast will populate as a result. If someone is searching for that celebrity and wants to hear an interview with them, they just might download your show and, if they enjoy the interview, listen to more of your podcasts and become a subscriber.

Celebrities don't automatically make your show successful or generate tons of downloads.

You also may get more eyes on your website and ears listening to your podcast if you have celebrity guests because people are impressed when they see that you landed a "big name guest." However, the challenge then becomes keeping those new listeners beyond the first "wow" moment with the celebrity as the headline.

There's quite a misconception among podcasters who believe that if they interview a celebrity, that celebrity will share the show with their huge audience and following and that the podcast, in turn, will get tons of new downloads. However, the truth is that most celebrities do not share their interviews as broadly or as frequently as the lesser known guests do. Celebrities are often interviewed several times a week and sometimes they are doing back-to-back interviews throughout the day. As a result, most of them do not share every single interview they do. It would be obnoxious if every day, several times a day they posted on social media about the number of times they were spotlighted.

Celebrities, or the publicists or agents who schedule their interviews, will also want to know about download numbers. If you only have 100 downloads per episode, it's probably not worth their time. If you have huge numbers, share that up front and you're more likely to get a "yes" to the interview request. If you don't want to share download numbers or you haven't launched yet, tell them how big your list is. If the list has 40,000 prospects, that gets attention. I use this strategy with my clients who haven't yet launched... but you have to have the list. Chances are you don't.

If these cold hard facts about celebrities bum you out, remember that your priority should be focused on bringing value to your listeners and not on using someone else's following to grow your own following.

Besides the fact the celebrities typically don't promote on your behalf after the interview, another downside to interviewing celebrities is that they are interviewed... **All.The.Time!** When someone is interviewed dozens of times a week, they tend to give canned answers and sound bored because, well, they've been getting interviewed a lot, so it does become boring for them. When someone is on a book tour, they are often asked the same questions repeatedly, so their answers can start to sound scripted. Michael O'Neal, host of *The Solopreneur Hour*, enjoys interviewing celebrities; however, he has one big stipulation. They must do the full hour, and he will not ask the same scripted questions that every other show is asking them.

As a listener, I enjoy listening to podcasts with guests that I have never heard of that are hosted by podcasters I know, like, and trust. Every episode is a new treat with value I have not yet received on any other podcast. This is why I highly recommend that you focus on finding and booking guests who are new to your community. There are several pros and not as many cons to interviewing guests who are lesser known in your industry.

A lesser known guest of brings a lot of freshness to answers since they have not been repeatedly interviewed. That adds interest and value to your show!

The first big benefit to interviewing guests who are not as well-known is that they likely have not been interviewed that much on other podcasts. The result? They are more likely to share your podcast with their own communities! Rather than feeling like they're doing you a favor by gracing you with their presence, they express a lot of gratitude for inviting them on to your show and, in turn, promote the podcast more heavily on social media. It benefits you both!

Lesser known guests also deliver more raw interviews. In other words, their responses sound very fresh because they are. Since they are not being interviewed several times per day or week, every question you ask them is fresh to them, so their answers do not come off as scripted. This adds a great deal of value to your podcast and your audience.

When you book a celebrity guest, you likely have to cut through a lot of red tape before scheduling the interview. There are assistants, managers, and publicists to convince before you ever actually talk to the guest. Michael Hyatt, host of *This Is Your Life* and a very well-known blogger and entrepreneur, rarely accepts interview invitations from podcasters. He has shared on his podcast that he wants to say yes to everyone, but his schedule simply does not allow for him to say yes to everyone requesting him. So Michael has his assistant review all requests. He said his assistant is much better at saying no than he is!

What I've learned after requesting Michael Hyatt as a guest for several of my clients' podcasts, and many other guests like him, is that my email will never even get in front of him or a similarly well-known guest. An assistant will read and reply with a "Thanks, but no thanks" because their priority is protecting their client's time. When you request an interview with a lesser known guest, there is a much higher chance that your email and invitation will actually be read and replied to by the guest themselves.

Are you new to podcasting? If so, chances are you are not that good yet. I hate to break it to you, but becoming a great interviewer takes a lot of practice. It is much better to "practice" your interviewing and honing interview skills with guests who aren't the A-list celebrities. Your guests will be peers who are quicker to forgive when you forget to record the interview and need to reschedule. Your guests will be peers who don't mind when you stumble over your words and need to re-start a sentence. Your guests will be peers who are quick to help you by introducing you to new people and referring clients to you.

I'm not suggesting that celebrity guests won't help you in these ways, but when I book very well-known guests on podcasts with hosts who make any of the aforementioned mistakes, they are usually aggravated and irritated for their time being wasted, not understanding and not being very, if at all, forgiving.

It's a matter of learning to walk before you run.

#ROCKTHEPODCAST Recap:

- *When you use the interview format for your podcast, you ease your own burden of developing content. Plus, interviews lead to relationships and podcasting is all about relationship marketing.*

- *Twitter is one of the best social media platforms on which to find guests. Unlike Facebook, on Twitter you can gain more immediate access to initiate a conversation.*

- *Twitter also makes suggestions about similar people who may interest you, so you can let the Twitter algorithm do more of the work of finding appropriate guests.*

- *Amazon started as a book store! Search there for guests because authors with recently released books on topics that provide value to your audience make great guests.*

- *Your guest will reflect on your show, so do your homework to qualify them prior to booking. Listen to other podcasts they have done or watch videos they have produced.*

- *While you must do your homework in advance, don't allow your show to be entirely scripted or it comes off as boring.*

- *Take charge of introducing your guest. As the host, you are ideally positioned to build up excitement about the person you're about to interview. Don't simply read the bio they provided.*

Interview Connections

❖ *Interviewing is more than asking questions – there's an art and craft to a good interview. Keep listening and learning to improve your show.*

❖ *There are pros and cons to booking celebrities. Don't automatically presume that a celebrity will make your show successful. "No names" can bring a lot of value!*

Leveraging the Power of Guest Interviews

CHAPTER SEVEN:
HOW TO MONETIZE & MARKET

Most podcasters I know (myself included!) absolutely love podcasting. It's more than a marketing strategy to us, it is an art. It is a hobby that helps us grow our businesses and build our brands. But the kids need food and a roof over their heads, right?! So let's talk about how to make your podcast something that actually generates revenue in your business. After all, podcasting is a marketing strategy, and marketing strategies are in place to generate sales and revenue for your business and ultimately boost your bottom line.

There are a lot of marketers online and marketing consultants who are teaching podcasters various formulas to monetize their podcasts, but I advise against following someone else's formula. Podcasting is about ten years old as I write this book. When it comes to using podcasting as a marketing tool, however, we're still in the Wild, Wild West. Most top podcasts on iTunes with tens upon thousands of downloads are very different. There are tight 20-minute shows, long form two-hour interviews, and everything in between. There is no science or formula to growing an audience and monetizing your show.

Once again, what is comes down to is producing a high quality show with compelling content that people are attracted to and love so much that they share it with their own audiences, followers, and others. Dave Jackson, host of *The School of Podcasting*, gave an amazing presentation at Podfest in February 2016 during which he talked about how compelling content is the most critical aspect of growing a great podcast.

If this advice – compelling content for growth – sounds familiar, that's not surprising. It is the same advice for a good website and anything that occurs in the digital realm. Content is king.

When you are desperate to monetize your podcast, your listeners can tell! Years ago, I directed a door-to-door field canvass for a nonprofit organization, and my staff and I knocked on doors (cold calls!) asking for signatures on a petition as well as for donations. Each night we were accountable to raise $150 in checks or cash contributions. Our jobs depended on it. We knocked on doors from 4:30 to 9:00 p.m. When 8:00 rolled around and we only had $25 in donations with $125 to go until quota, we got stressed! We used to say, "You have dollar signs in your eyes" when someone became desperate for donations. The same thing will happen when you become overly desperate to monetize your podcast immediately. Remember, as I have stressed from the beginning of this book: Podcasting is long-term marketing. It will not generate an immediate payoff.

Most podcasters believe that they will get sponsors after growing a large audience of thousands of downloads per episode. How do they think they'll get more downloads? iTunes rankings! How do they think they'll get higher in the rankings? Subscriptions, ratings, and reviews! So, how does this desperation I just mentioned shine through in a podcast? It happens when the host spends too much time in each and every episode begging their listeners to go to iTunes to subscribe, rate, and review. This can, at times, sound annoying and desperate. It is especially bothersome to your listeners who already are subscribed and have already rated and reviewed. Asking them to do so is wasting their time.

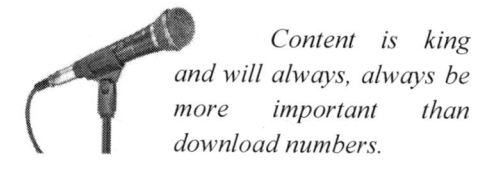

Content is king and will always, always be more important than download numbers.

I am sure there are podcasters who will disagree with this perspective. However, I believe it is far more important to keep your dedicated and subscribed listeners happy. When I listen to podcasts that I subscribe to every week, I am fully aware that there are a lot of other people also listening who may not be listening religiously every week. Regardless, when I listen to a podcast, the only two or three people in that room are me, and the people on the podcast (i.e. host and guest). Every week when the host asks me to subscribe, rate, and review I want to scream: "I ALREADY DID. STOP REMINDING ME!"

I think you can catch my drift. First rule of monetizing: don't be annoying. I understand that there may be (and certainly hopefully *are*) new listeners to your podcast and that you will want those people to subscribe, rate, and review, and there's one simple way to get those new listeners to take those actions without annoying your existing audience with your request. The one single thing that will get listeners to subscribe, rate, and review is a really good show. One with value for them. When I hear a really good show that has content I enjoy and that's funny, entertaining, and informative, the first thing I do is subscribe because I don't want to miss out. I don't subscribe because the host asked (or even told) me to.

Focus on producing a really good show. Otherwise, no matter how often you ask, plead, or implore listeners to subscribe, they are not going to. In fact, without a good show, chances are very good they will not listen a second time, and without a good show, sponsors are never going to knock on your door and ask to sponsor your show. Focus on a producing quality show and offering value – whether that value is in the form of education or entertainment.

Moving on.

Indirect Monetization

Contrary to popular belief, sponsorships and advertisements are not the only way you can monetize your podcast! In fact, if you currently have a business and your podcast is related to your business, I do not recommend that you take on third-party advertisers. By doing so, you will be directing your listeners' attention away from your business.

If you provide valuable content to your target market via your podcast, then you will drive targeted leads to your website. If you have a well-designed website with an opt-in form, you can convert those leads on to your email list and nurture them into paying clients.

There are four main steps to monetizing your podcast indirectly:
1. Create compelling content that is valuable to your target market.
2. Get listeners to your website.
3. Get them to opt in to your email list.
4. Nurture your relationship with them, so they become a client or customer.

Easier said than done! So let's look at it step by step.

Step 1: Create compelling content that is valuable to your target market.

Before you can even successfully complete this step, you must know who your target market is. Be specific and clear about who your show is for and who it is not for. Don't obsess over your download stats, but do track them so you can see which episodes are more popular and which aren't. When you see a spike in downloads for a particular topic or guest, you know you should do more of that kind of show! Also, keep an eye on how many comments or how much engagement you get on certain topics, so you know the type of content your audience likes the most.

If you aren't getting a lot of engagement… ask for it! Find one person who listens to your podcast and ask them for their feedback. Don't know anyone who listens? Pick someone who is in your target audience and ask them to listen, then ask for their feedback.

Step 2: Get listeners to your website.

Most listeners consume podcasts through a mobile device. They listen while they're driving, going for a walk, doing dishes, or exercising. In short, they aren't always sitting in front of a computer when they're listening and even when and if they are, they're typically working or doing other things, so visiting your website isn't something they can do at that moment.

In order to get listeners to visit your website, there must be a clear, strong, and easy-to-understand call to action that they *will remember*!

Your call to action must be *clear*: What are you offering to the listener if they visit your website? Is the value clearly defined? If it's a special report or give away of some sort, does it clearly relate to the value you just shared in the podcast episode?

Your call to action must be *strong*: As I said before, "strength" makes me picture someone (or something) who is confident, who cannot be easily pushed over, and who knows that the value they have and their purpose is rock solid and irrefutable. Is your call to action something that is irresistible to listeners? When you state your call to action, is the tone in your voice communicating the fact that you *know* without a doubt that your offer *will* help that listener?

Your call to action must be *easy to understand*: Whatever your call to action is, make it super easy to understand! As I said before, if your URL is really long, create an easy link that shortens it. Again, in your call to action, there should only be *one step*. Do not ask listeners to visit this website, go to that social media page, and send you an email. Give them one clear instruction to act on.

Step 3: Get them to opt in to your email list.

There are entire books on website conversions, so this is a tough step to fit into a few short paragraphs! Adam Hommey, founder of Help My Website Sell, gave a lot of helpful tips to my audience during our interview on *Rhodes to Success*. (My interview with Adam was so full of great information about this topic, that I've included the transcription of it in the Resource section at the end of this book!)

Simply getting traffic to your website is not all it takes; you actually need visitors who are prequalified, prepped, and pumped:

- Prequalified: You're addressing the right people. (See step 1 and be certain you clearly understand who your target audience is.)
- Prepped: Listeners and prospects know what to expect when they get to your website.
- Pumped: They are excited to be there, so they are eagerly waiting for the page to load to take action.

It could take up to a year or more before someone actually contacts you after they first hear about you, so keep delivering valuable content and keep giving your listeners clear calls to action and keep yourself top of mind with subsequent marketing "touches."

Step 4: Nurture your relationship with them, so they become a client or customer.

In this step, we are getting deeper into email marketing tips and moving beyond podcast tips, but if you want to see results with podcast interviews, you need more than a great interview. You need a marketing funnel set up, so when a listener joins your email list, they don't turn around and unsubscribe or ignore your emails.

Remember: Podcasting is relationship marketing. The whole point is to enable you to create deeper relationships and more revenue as a result.

Here are a couple of simple steps to take with your email marketing. First, an email should be sent immediately and automatically, delivering your free gift and welcoming them to your community. Then, a sequence of 10 to 12 emails over the course of a month should be dripped to them with a ton of value. These emails should be conversational in nature and provide value, value, and more value. One tip I've learned and implemented is to end each email with something like, "I will touch base in a few days to check in!" You can also say, "Reply to this email and answer this question." This will inspire people to engage with you and allow you to learn who your listeners are!

Another tip you can implement is to set up a tripwire. A tripwire is a small offering that new subscribers can buy. My tripwire is my e-book and one sheet template for $6.97. Several times a week, I see orders come through of new list subscribers who took action on my tripwire offer. Not only are they getting my email sequence, but now I have their mailing address. What do I do with that? I add them to my print newsletter list and they hear from me once a month in their mailbox at their house or P.O. box!

You need to invest in more than a good podcast or good interview. You need to focus on your email marketing, your social media marketing, your offline marketing, and more. By doing so, when someone hears you on a podcast and they join your email list or your social media community, there is content and conversation happening that will motivate them to invest in your products or services.

It's not as easy to measure how much money you make indirectly with your podcast than if you were to have advertisers paying you directly for air time (a very easy metric to measure), but it could potentially be much, much more.

So remember, as an entrepreneur your podcast is a great way to provide value to your audience, attract a following, and capture leads who can turn into paying clients. Sponsors are not the only way you can monetize your podcast.

Direct Monetization

To directly monetize your show, you need to get a business to sponsor it or advertise on your podcast. A lot of the major podcasts on iTunes use a company called Midroll to acquire sponsors. However, Midroll does have pretty high standards. You should have at least 15,000 downloads per episode, if not more, to be considered for their service. Even if you do not use their service, if you use the old "CPM" model which means cost per thousand downloads, you need a pretty large audience to make a good income from your show. A lot of shows make $25 per thousand downloads. If I used this model, I wouldn't make very much money directly from my podcast!

It is important to keep in mind that podcasts are not radio! The CPM model is dated and does not need to be used when getting sponsors or advertisers for your show. Businesses will want to sponsor a podcast that puts them in front of their own target markets. I know a lot of podcasters who monetize their shows with sponsors, and they have never shared their download stats!

If you want to approach a business and successfully secure them as a sponsor for your show, keep in mind the following:

- Be very clear about who your target audience is and make sure your content supports that. For example, my target audience is podcasters and people interested in being a guest on podcasts, so I focus my episodes on topics related to podcasters and being a podcast guest expert.
- Identify businesses that have services or products that your target audience wants and needs.
- Reach out to those businesses with a pitch!

It is probably a good idea to have a media kit that shows the potential sponsor your audience size, history of the show, your rates, etc. but I don't think it's completely necessary. If you approach businesses that you know and most importantly businesses that **know you**, a friendly email and phone call broaching the subject can result in a very successful sale!

Corey Coates and I co-host *The Podcast Producers*. We are laser focused on who our target audience is and our content reflects that. After we dropped Season 1, one company approached us and wanted to sponsor! When Season 2 was approaching, we decided that Podcast Movement would be the perfect business to advertise on our show. We have a great relationship with the founders and both my business, Interview Connections, and Corey's business, Podfly, had already invested in booths at their annual conference.

I sent the following email:

Hi Jared and Dan,
It was great seeing you both at Podfest! Really looking forward to PM16!
Corey and I had a productive planning meeting for Season 2 of The Podcast Producers *over some wine at Podfest, and the production is under way! We will be producing eight episodes, each featuring a conversation with us and an experienced podcaster(s). Season 2 will be the "behind the music" for podcasters. It will be fun, entertaining, and of course, informative. We will be releasing our shows twice monthly with the season finale on July 5th (just in time for PM!)*
I'm reaching out to see if you're open to a conversation about Podcast Movement sponsoring Season 2 of The Podcast Producers.
We don't have a fancy media kit, and if you're open to it, I'd love to hop on the phone.
In the meantime, I'll give you some info upfront:
The Season 2 cast of characters:
-Liz Covart of Ben Franklin's World
-Harry Duran of Podcast Junkies
-Katie and Chris Krimitsos of Biz Women Rock *and* Podfest
-Natalie Eckdahl of Biz Chix
-Glenn the Geek of Horse Radio Network
-Dave Jackson of School of Podcasting
-Jason and Karen of The Walking Dead 'Cast
-Elsie and Jess of She Podcasts
Season 1 had about 1,500 downloads per episode with high engagement from our fans.
Our raw and uncut interviews averaged 300 to 500 downloads each.
Our pitch is $<redacted>* for the whole season; flat rate.
Let me know what you think!
Jessica

(* Please understand I redacted the cost of their sponsorship as that amount is not public.)

Did you notice anything about this email? Let's break it down. I was friendly but got right to the point. I asked for a phone call early on but with a direct ask; we never had to negotiate over the phone. I listed our guests, so they knew who they would be helping to promote as well. I did give a snapshot of downloads, but we did not sell them on a CPM model. While I'm not sharing how much they paid, I will say the amount was a no brainer.

Start small and be certain that a prospective sponsor is the right fit for your show and audience.

Which brings me to my last point: If you're starting out and haven't gotten a sponsor yet, start with a low ask! Once they see results with your show, raise your prices. Sponsoring podcasts is a new advertising venue for so many businesses. It is risky and business owners don't want to roll the dice and lose a lot of money. Make the investment a no brainer and you will get sponsors for your show.

Podcast Advertising

So while a lot of podcasters don't believe in the CPM model, it's really important to keep in mind that it may be what the advertisers or sponsors want. In terms of direct monetization of your podcast, the advertiser is your customer, so you have to satisfy them. However (and this is a pretty big however), you must be comfortable with both the product or service that is being presented as your sponsor and how well if fits into your show.

On our show, *The Podcast Producers*, Corey Coates and I interviewed a number of podcasters as well as the pros who bring podcasters and advertisers together (like Midroll representatives) and uncovered a lot of interesting facts about podcast advertising.

If there is money to be made ***directly*** from a podcast, that occurs through advertising. That said, it's also very important to realize that only a very, very small percentage of podcasts are making money due to advertising. One of our interviewees estimated that only about 20 to 30 podcasts are generating revenue *simply* from advertising.

The attraction to podcast advertising tends to be rooted in the typical podcast audience. Listeners tend to be middle to upper middle class and tech savvy. Tech savviness usually brings with it disposable income. Podcast listeners want free, and they understand that for the podcast to be free, it needs to be supported by advertising. Because of that, listeners are willing to check out the advertisers of their favorite podcasts. They want to buy to support the show... and get cool products. In addition to a higher level of tech savviness, podcast listeners are also higher than normal on the "cool" scale.

We also uncovered that podcast advertising is proving itself to be effective. Direct response advertisers are more astute about advertising dollars and returns on investment (ROI) than almost any other advertising professional or type of media buyer. They watch every dollar spent and track every response to be able to prove and cite ROIs. When the direct response advertiser renews podcast advertising, you can bet that it's working. These folks are watching the metrics closely and reviewing them with a fine-tooth comb. And these folks are, in fact, renewing. With that, advertisers are now coming to podcasters to ask them to lend *their* credibility to the product or service.

While it may be nice to be pursued by an advertiser, you absolutely must pick and choose what works for your podcast! Another podcaster told us that he had sponsors approaching him in the first month after launch, but he said that he picks and chooses very, very carefully who he will accept as an advertiser, no matter what the money may be. This is very sage advice. Remember, you are tacitly endorsing your advertisers and vice versa. It has to make sense for your audience and be the right fit.

In addition to being the right fit for your show, you have to be comfortable reading and voicing the advertisement. You have veto rights because it's your show. In that sense, podcasters are weeding out the ads that they know their listeners don't want to hear anyway. They know their audiences want "cool," so that's what they pursue. This in turn increases the effectiveness of the advertisements they accept.

Good delivery of the ad read is what makes listeners want to check it out. The read becomes interesting and fun and connects with the audience. An inline read (i.e. reading a script) is difficult for most podcasters to pull off. Your audience will hear in your voice if you really believe what you're saying, and they'll know if you're reading a script or speaking from the heart. If it's not from your heart, the audience won't buy into the ad. You need to explain why you think the product or service is a great deal for them, so you truly have to believe it in the first place!

You have to fully believe in the product or service you're promoting. If not, your audience will see right through it.

Advertisers also tend to prefer this approach: having the podcaster talk about the product/service in the flow of the show rather than having it set apart as an obvious advertisement. Listeners are also becoming more attuned to advertising in the podcasts they enjoy. They know when they're hearing a paid ad, so make it worth their while and something in which they will get value... or at least entertainment. Knowing that, it's a better approach to ask an advertiser for a bullet point list rather than a written script to give you more room to discuss the product/service more naturally. Also ask for a list of what not to say. There have been times when a podcaster, speaking off the cuff, said something that didn't mesh with what the advertiser really wanted.

Using a Webinar to Monetize Your Podcast

A webinar, a pre-recorded (or even live) web-based seminar or presentation in which you present value to the listening audience – exactly like you do in your podcast – can also be a way to monetize and market your podcast. A webinar is much like a lecture but with the opportunity for a call to action or sales opportunity at the end. Webinars are automatable and, when recorded, can be repeated with no extra effort from you. They are also one of the best ways to convert prospects into clients and existing clients into higher-paying clients.

Once you have been podcasting for a while, you won't have much of a learning curve for the technical aspects of producing a webinar. You really don't need to worry about creating a flashy PowerPoint presentation. Steven Essa, known internationally as the "make money with webinars expert," has conducted a lot of research regarding webinar presentation and is discovering that simple black and white information is as effective as more complex graphics. In fact, simple black and white slides may be more effective since they seem more educational and less sales-y.

While you don't sell during your podcast, you can sell on the webinar. That opportunity occurs at the end. You might offer pricing that is only available to webinar participants or otherwise offer a special call to action to give attendees something of value. Start your webinar by immediately outlining the benefit for your listeners. Tell them why they should listen and why you want to talk to *them*. Reiterate that you are a credible source with case studies, statistics, and testimonials. Keep in mind that when you offer special or reduced pricing, you have to have a reason. You need to provide practical, actionable steps that participants can take away.

Whether or not you choose to monetize your podcast either directly via advertising or if you choose to market it via any of the ways we've covered, one thing remains the same: You have to love what you're doing and be passionate about what you are discussing and covering in your podcast. That will always come through loud and clear and, even without sponsors or advertisers, will underscore your expertise. That expertise serves to drive revenue in your core business. Yes, there are some instances in which the podcast became *the business*, but those are rare. Your podcast is part of your overall long-term marketing strategy for your core business. If you can generate a few bucks (or more) to help offset its production cost, great. But don't lose sight of the big picture!

Podcast Marketing

Before we start talking about ways in which you can market your podcast, let's not lose sight of the fact that you've started your podcast to ***market your business***. Almost all podcasters begin that way: podcasting to show your expertise in your niche and to talk about what you are most passionate. The podcast will almost never become a primary revenue model. In fact, most podcasters start without a plan in place to monetize it at all.

A lot of people focus on growing their download numbers, and many ask me how big the audience should be and what good download numbers are. My answer is always the same: It depends. It depends on what your goal is for the show and what you want to do with it in terms of driving your core business. Larger download numbers are not necessarily the solution. In fact, the reality is, they may not even matter.

You simply do not need big numbers. Listenership is lower, but conversion is higher because you are speaking directly to your target audience. It goes back to the adage: Better to be a big fish in a little pond than a little fish in a big one. I know a lot of podcasters who get too focused on trying to grow their numbers rather than paying attention to the listeners they already have. Nurture the relationships you have now with people who have *already* opted in and are subscribers to your podcast. Those are the people who are going to ultimately generate the most revenue for you.

I recently worked with a prospect who was very concerned about audience statistics. He had a cool new product but was convinced he had to get in front of a large audience. I showed him how he could get on four shows with average audiences of 200 each as a podcast guest expert and close one deal that would more than double his investment with Interview Connections. It's about the conversion rate, not the download numbers.

So, on to marketing your podcast.

As with promoting the interviews on which you are featured as a podcast guest expert, social media provides a solid venue for podcast marketing. However, you can't simply post and promote shows on social media when you release them in order to get the results you want. That type of blatant self-promotion never goes very far at all. People turn to social media for engagement, not advertising.

With social media, think about building a community not an audience. I interviewed Katie Krimitsos who hosts the podcast, *Biz Women Rock,* on my podcast, *Rhodes to Success.* She shared how she used Facebook to begin promoting her podcast before it even launched. She chose Facebook over Twitter or even LinkedIn (which might have made more sense for her audience) because she loves Facebook. That's the first point about using social media – choose the platform that you enjoy! Katie also paid for Facebook ads to get in front of as many of her target audience members (female entrepreneurs) as possible.

It pays to have someone who really understands Facebook advertising (or advertising on the platform of your choice) to generate the results you want. In Katie's case, she was spending about $3.00 to $5.00 a day and was getting the number of likes she wanted; however, she also knew that likes aren't the end of the game. Likes, shares, and comments lead to engagement, and engagement is what you really want. Without engagement, social media is a dead end for your podcast marketing.

To boost engagement, you might also consider starting a group on Facebook or whatever social media you choose. Keep in mind that a group needs to be monitored to be effective and to keep group members returning and engaging with one another, so think about reaching out to your network and even some of your best clients to become brand ambassadors for you. In this role, these people will help keep the conversation flowing on social media. They post and help answer questions to maintain interest and activity. You don't even have to offer them anything other than leadership and their own exposure.

Glenn the Geek, founder of *Horse Radio Network*, also shared his insights regarding marketing podcasts when I interviewed him on *Rhodes to Success*. He started with zero listeners and one show and has grown that into thousands and thousands of listeners with about a dozen different shows on his network. Glenn's show started years ago, before podcasting was as mainstream as it is now, and it was geared toward horse lovers who weren't very tech savvy at the time. It was an extremely niched audience who not only wanted to listen, but who went out of their way to figure out *how* to listen. This really speaks to the importance of quality content.

Social media works well for marketing your podcast, but remember social media is about engagement!

Glenn got his first sponsor after about three to six months... when he had a whopping total of 12 listeners! How? He knew he had the niche (the 20 percent who would be responsible for 80 percent of the sales) for the right sponsor. He found a growing company and simply asked. He didn't worry about CPM (and admits he didn't even know what that was for years). Instead, he offered a small rate to sponsor the show. To this day, he still doesn't have huge numbers to sell, but he knows he has the right audience and that his podcasts will help sponsors grow their own brands over time. It's a mutually beneficial relationship – Glenn helps them grow and they help him grow.

Approach those businesses that make sense for your show and your audience. Consider a flat rate per show or some sort of alternate advertising. Think outside the box. Successful podcasts don't need to follow the CPM model (as Glenn proved) due to having niche audiences and small but perfectly targeted numbers. Create a package that may include a banner ad on the page or to offer additional promotion via social media. Perhaps you will want to use give away prizes that are sponsored. Know your audience demographics, then think of companies that want to get in front of that audience.

Target mid-size and smaller companies to create a mutually beneficial relationship in which you will help each other grow. Make the sponsor part of your show also by including them in the content in some way. Perhaps it even makes sense to interview a company representative as a guest expert. Ask them to sponsor a segment of the show, like "tips of the week" or something similar.

The best way to market your show is to simply ask. Show what you have to offer and how sponsoring a show will help your advertising prospect. Talk to everyone in your network who has a logical connection to your podcast. Trade shows in your industry are also excellent places to look for sponsors. For example, you could become the radio network for the tradeshow or an industry association. Don't think you're big enough to call yourself a network? Glenn started his network with only one show. He explains, "We just made it up, and it started with one show." If you need to, go back and re-read the chapter about positioning yourself as a celebrity!

Podcast Discoverability

Whether you are a podcast guest expert or are hosting your own show, you want to be discovered. You will also want to discover other podcasts on which you can be interviewed as a guest expert or those with which you can possibly connect your own show (e.g. hosts interviewing each other).

In searching for podcasts, iTunes is the logical place and a great place to start. That said, keep in mind that when you search on a keyword or keyword phrase in iTunes, you will get returns that seem to have nothing to do with the search word or phrase you used. When that occurs, start with a broad category and browse and sort from there.

My team and I spend a great deal of time in the iTunes store, and as an entrepreneur using podcasting as a marketing strategy, you will, too. The iTunes store has about 15 different categories of podcasts and within each of those there are sub categories. Categories include arts, business, education, games and hobbies, health, music, sports and recreations, etc. The number of sub categories depends on the parent category. For example, there are currently seven sub categories under arts (design, fashion and beauty, food, literature, performing arts, spoken word, and visual arts); however, there are dozens of sub categories under music… as you would expect. Once you get to this level, iTunes will present sub collections including New and Noteworthy, What's Hot, Top Podcasts, Top Episodes, and All Podcasts.

Yes, I am specifically talking about ***browsing*** podcasts here as opposed to friends or colleagues referring them, but there are listeners who do, in fact, browse for podcasts to listen to. Don't overlook that.

As with perusing books on Amazon, there is artwork involved with podcasts on iTunes. Although podcasts are clearly auditory, the initial introduction may be the visual representation via your podcast artwork in the iTunes store. Some will teach that podcast artwork has to be yellow in order to get attention; however, there is no tried and true formula for creating attention-getting artwork. Go to What's Hot and you will see podcast artwork in every color. Your artwork needs to grab the attention of your ideal listener and be relatively descriptive regarding the overall topic of your show. While a graphic may be completely clever, if it doesn't easily convey to the potential listener what they're going to get when they listen, it becomes useless.

Likewise, your podcast title should be descriptive rather than cute. As with the subject line of an email, your prospective listener has to be attracted enough to click on it. The show title and overall presence on iTunes needs to be attractive to the audience... and it needs to make sense. I see many who forgo clarity about the show for cleverness, and those shows are often overlooked by the very listeners the show host is looking for.

You will also create a show description. Let me warn you right now that trying to stuff your description full of keywords to try to game the iTunes system won't work. At this point, the search algorithm in iTunes isn't that great. Depending on key words used in the search, the results may or just as easily may not be what the searcher is looking for. Rather than worry about key words and SEO, instead your description should be very clear to potential listeners and include:

- What the show is about
- The goal of the podcast
- Who is listening (your target audience and ideal listener)

You should also include a list of episodes, and those titles are as important as the show title and need to describe what each podcast episode is about. Title them correctly! That title should describe what the podcast is about. If you have a celebrity guest expert, you can include that, but it doesn't work very well for "no names."

Keep in mind that there is limited space in iTunes for the episode title. Some podcasters believe you should include the episode number, but that may only make sense for a serialized show. Due to space limitations, you may want to forgo the episode number.

Once a prospective listener finds your show and is drawn to a particular episode and clicks "play," you have about three minutes to capture and keep that listener's attention. I've heard a lot of podcasters take way too long to get to the point of the podcast episode, so listeners click "stop" and never return to the episode or the show. These podcasters don't grab attention from the start. That is probably the biggest reasons a listener will click "stop" and not return. You must also balance your introductory comments between veteran and brand new listeners. And as I said before, don't lead the podcast by asking listeners to rate and review! Give them a quality show to rate and review by getting right into the meat of the topic or interview. Get to the point! Give them a good show.

#ROCKTHEPODCAST Recap:

- *It's all about content, content, content. That is what drives the success of any podcast!*

- *You need to cater to your existing audience, so don't bore them (or worse, aggravate them) with repeated pleas to subscribe, rate, and review.*

- *Indirect monetization that ultimately sends listeners to your website and on to your list so you can develop and nurture a relationship is difficult to quantify; however, this indirect monetization has the potential for far greater payoffs than sponsorships and advertisements.*

- *Don't get stuck worrying about the CPM model. It's quickly becoming outdated. A simple flat rate or your own creative advertising package works better.*

- *Direct response advertisers are very astute regarding advertising effectiveness, and they are renewing their podcast ads. That only means one thing: It works!*

- *Before you accept a sponsor or advertisement, you must be certain it makes sense for your show and that you are 100 percent comfortable with it and truly believe in the product or service.*

- *Social media platforms work well to market your podcast; however, social media is all about engagement. You can't simply post and promote your show.*

- *Make sure your presence in the iTunes stores clearly reflects and describes your show and each episode.*

- *Consider using a webinar to both monetize and promote your podcast and your business.*

PART 3:
YOUR PODCASTING MINDSET

CHAPTER EIGHT:
PODCASTING TO ACTUALLY GROW YOUR BUSINESS

Now that we've covered each side of the mic, it's time to consider **both** sides of it in order to grow your business and having the right mindset about podcasting as a marketing tool.

Here's a question I get quite a lot from my clients: "Should I host my own show, or be a guest on other people's podcasts?" My answer is always, "Both!" It's simply a matter of what you decide to do first.

Being a guest expert on podcasts in which you can speak to your target market is a great way to get more people listening to your show because if they're listening to a podcast, you know they are auditory learners. If you promote your podcast on a blog, it's hard to tell if the reader is someone who enjoys consuming content in audio form as well.

There are several reasons why it is important to be both a podcast host and a podcast guest expert:

1. When you get booked as a guest, you can also interview that host on your show and deepen the relationship with them. This shows your gratitude and makes that host more likely to promote your interview on their own podcast.
2. You become a much better guest expert when you host your own show because you know what it takes to produce a podcast. Producing a podcast is hard work! I was interviewed a lot as a guest before I started my own show, and let me tell you, my guest appearances have improved dramatically since I also became a host. I now fully understand the other side.

3. Podcast listeners who hear your appearances as a guest expert and enjoy your content will want to get more from you! As people who like listening to podcasts, they're much more likely to "join your community" by way of subscribing to your podcast. If you only write a blog or record videos, people who listen to podcasts as their preferred method of content consumption won't find much of your content because it's not in the format that they prefer.

As you can quickly discern, there are real benefits to sitting on both sides of the mic as a means of growing your core business. Whether you start as a podcast guest expert or by hosting your own show, there is a learning curve and an investment. Once you've covered that, why not leverage it to a great degree by being on both sides of the mic. It makes all the sense in the world.

The astute entrepreneur will always want to know if podcasting is worth their time. When Chris Spurvey interviewed me on *It's Time to Sell*, he asked, "I keep hearing that everyone is listening to podcasts. Is it true?" Chris asked because he was intrigued about the idea of being booked as a podcast guest expert and wanted to know if it would be worth pursuing and worth his time. "Are people really listening and is this worth my time?"

You probably think my answer was a resounding, "Yes, everyone is listening to podcasts!" However, I was honest with him then and I'll be equally honest with you right now: No, not everyone is listening to podcasts. The statistic of podcast listeners is indeed growing and perhaps may be as high as 60 percent as I write this; however, that statistic is a bit irrelevant. What matters is the number of people who are in your target audience who are listening to a podcast on which you might appear as a guest expert and the number listening to your own podcast. Here's the harsh, make-no-bones-about-it reality: It is not a lot of people. Not a lot of people will likely be listening to the podcast on which you might be interviewed. In fact, according to Rob Walsh from Libsyn (media host company): If you publish a podcast episode and a month later have 150 to 175 downloads, you have more downloads than 50 percent of the podcasts on iTunes. The reality is podcast audiences are small.

But that's not a bad thing!

The important thing to remember and know is that the audiences you are addressing are highly targeted and very niche. While there may only be 200 downloads for the episode on which you appear as a podcast guest expert, that's okay. It's the audience make up that matters most. I have some clients who tell me that the minimum download stat for podcasts on which they'll agree to be booked is 1,000. It's fine to have that as a standard; however, if you adopt that standard as well, it severely limits the number of shows you'll appear on.

Reality is that podcast audiences are small. But, most importantly, these audiences are very targeted!

The other thing to keep in mind is that download stats are not public. The only people who truly know how many downloads a podcast has are those people who can access the media host. So that's usually the podcast host and perhaps the editor and producer. As a podcast guest expert, there is no way for you to verify how many downloads a podcast has. So that begs the question: How do you know if a podcast is worth the investment of your time? You're spending time and money to be booked on a podcast, so you want there to be a payoff of some sort. You want there to be a return on your investment. I completely understand. You don't want to be on a show with only a single listener... unless that listener is your perfect client and can write you a big check.

The thing you want to focus on the most is relevancy of the content and whether or not the podcast target audience mirrors your own business's target audience. For example, on *Rhodes to*

Success, our target audience is podcasters, those interested in podcasts, people who want to be booked on podcasts, etc. The show has a focused tone and vibe about podcasting.

About a year ago, I interviewed my friend, Corey Coates (with whom I co-host *The Podcast Producers*) on my *Rhodes to Success* podcast. I'll be completely transparent and share that *Rhodes to Success* does not have thousands of downloads, yet Corey enjoyed positive results from the interview. There are a lot of shows on which he could have been interviewed that have 5,000 or 10,000 downloads. However, because Corey was in front of his perfect target audience and talking to my listeners who are podcasters, he got a lot of new, paying clients who had listened to that episode. Sure, he could have gone on a show with 10,000 downloads (and has), but if that podcast isn't geared toward his target audience, he would not get the same results and enjoy the high quality leads he got from my much-smaller-by-comparison show.

Here's what Corey shared with me about his experience: "I was on a show a while ago and this guy did everything right. He had the pre-interview one sheet, all the social media sharing, 10,000 to 20,000 listeners per episode, and he said, 'You being on my show is going to draw a ton of traffic and a lot of business for you, so get ready for the onslaught of inbound activity.'

"I did his show and was heavily tweeted about and shared on Facebook quite a bit about the show and interview, and I got absolutely ***zero*** calls, ***zero*** leads, ***no*** follow up, and one even contacted me saying, 'Hey I heard you on that show and really liked it.' Of the dozens of shows I've done, yours, Jessica, has earned me the greatest amount of inbound traffic and number of leads. It's simply because, not the size of your audience, but the way you engaged me in conversation and the way you engage your audience as the host. Very simply: Size doesn't always matter!"

I certainly appreciate Corey's comments about my show and my skill as a host, and I will reiterate that it's the makeup of the audience and not the size that matters. Don't just look for shows with high download numbers and do not equate download numbers with anticipated success. Look for shows on which you'll connect with the audience and build a relationship with the podcast host. Success comes from getting in front of the *right* audience, not necessarily a big audience.

Size Really Doesn't Matter

First, you have to have all of your ducks in a row regarding your marketing efforts. If you plan to grow your business as a podcast guest expert, you have to have a lot of other things in place in your business if you want the podcast interviews to help you gain traction. I never recommend that my clients use podcast interviews as a way to grow their businesses if they are very new and have very little on the back end to support the interview results. Certainly, if you're new, you can be a podcast guest expert to start to get exposure, but listeners are going to expect more from you than simply the interview. If you want to see results in terms of people signing up for your coaching program, buying your book, or subscribing to your own podcast, etc., you have to have things in place on the other side of the interview!

For example, you have to ensure you're speaking to the right audience, your content (the topic and questions you answer during the interview) has to be relevant to the audience, and you have to offer them some sort of value. You also need to have a call to action to close the interview that motivates listeners to visit your website, and when they get there, they find even more value to make them want to opt in to your mailing list, hang out on your website, read your blog, watch your videos, etc. You must have these things in place before the interview to increase the likelihood that listeners are going to want to connect and then stay connected with you. Without all of this set up and ready to go on the backend means your appearance as a podcast guest expert is a bit like

Podcasting to Actually Grow Your Business

shooting in the dark. You won't know where the bullets are landing.

I learned a similar lesson that I'll share with you as an analogy. During a recent beach vacation, I thought it would be fun to fly a kite with my 3-year-old son. Now I hadn't flown a kite in probably 15 years. We went to the store and found a kite shaped like a pirate ship with sails and, well, the works. We put it together and took it to the beach. There was plenty of wind, and I ran with it, getting it about two whopping feet off the ground. My son tried to run with it and ended up tripping over it and breaking it. Far from a successful venture despite how much wind there was and how fancy the kite was. So we found another kite at another store – simple, plain, nothing fancy, and "guaranteed to fly." The return trip to the beach was met with huge kite-flying success.

The same is true for you and your success with podcast interviews. Big and fancy (aka huge download numbers) is not a guarantee of success. Like me who was not ready to fly a big fancy pirate ship kite, if you aren't ready with all the other components, you'll likely flop. You must have all the parts in place in order for your interview to help you and your business soar. No matter how much wind there was on the beach that day, that pirate ship kite (in my hands without the skills) wasn't going any place. In the same manner, no matter how many listeners may hear your interview, if everything on the backend is not ready to go (e.g. your site is bad, your call to action stinks, and your content is irrelevant), you will not see results in your business.

Large download numbers are absolutely no guarantee of success! You must have the back end in place as well.

I recently interviewed my business coach who you'll remember is my dad, Jim Palmer. Jim has launched a number of online businesses including No Hassle Newsletters, No Hassle Social Media, Concierge Print and Mail Newsletters to name just a few. His current flagship business is Dream Business Coaching and Mastermind, and he hosts an annual live event, Dream Business Academy. Plus he has his own podcast, *Stick Like Glue Radio*. I actually started my business as a virtual assistant, and he was my first client. I worked to book him on podcasts, and to this day, he continues to appear on podcasts as a guest expert and fully understands that audience size doesn't matter.

When Jim uses Interview Connections to book him on shows, his concern is never the size of the audience or number of downloads. Instead, he focuses on whether or not the host is a good match for him. Regardless of the success he's had over the years, he is still using podcast interviews to grow his coaching business.

He explains: "One of the mistakes a lot of entrepreneurs make with podcast interviews or any marketing effort, for that matter, is being more concerned with 'what' rather than 'who.' A lot of clients want to only be on a big show, and that makes sense; however, it doesn't mean you have to be on a show with 10,000 or 15,000 downloads. If I were on a fairly new show with a great host that produces a great interview with only ten listeners, that's going to be good for business because even though one-to-many is a good marketing approach, ultimately all business is done one-to-one. All business is done through relationships with a single person.

"I do 12 interviews a month because I know that all I have to do is connect with one person per episode and it's a home run. That said, I ask to be booked on shows that are hosted by entrepreneurs who are using their podcast as a way to increase their own businesses or they're using the podcast as their business and want to grow their revenue stream. In either case, they're in growth mode and that's a great fit for me because that's what I do – help people grow their businesses. No matter if the host is experienced or a newbie, you want to make the host look really, really good. This is actually a learned skill. I've done a lot of interviews hosting my own show in which the interviewee makes it all about them. Every answer to a question either becomes about their website or some other self-promotion. There is no value for the listeners in this. In fact, over the years, there were probably three interviews I did that I never published because it was nothing but self-promotion.

"To make the host look good (especially the nervous new ones), before we start recording, I ask about their audience and what the host's goal is. I flat out ask them, 'How can I make this show successful for you?' Many hosts are blown away when I ask this question. While the content I share from show to show may be similar, I can tailor my answers more specifically to the particular audience whether that's new entrepreneurs, entrepreneurs trying to grow to the next level, folks who may be facing certain life challenges, etc. The more you can help the host have a great show, the better chance you'll have to really connect with their audience as well.

"I've also invited hosts to come on my own show, *Stick Like Glue Radio*. It's a great way to have a conversation and offer a lot of value. On a sales call, you're in sales mode. An interview on a podcast is often more like a job interview. I teach an aspect of this at Dream Business Academy and call it 'seed planting.' It's almost like covertly dropping information without coming across as being too sales-y. When someone asks me about creating videos, for example, I give valuable tips, but I preface those by mentioning, 'Well, that's something I teach at Dream Business Academy.' Plus there is usually time after the recording stops to have a personal conversation with the host, and I always ask, 'Was that good for you?' I also then begin asking them about their own business. The host just heard me for 30 minutes or so and has seen my bio, etc., so it's more important for me to

On the most successful shows, both the guest expert and host make each other look good.

understand what their business is to determine if I can help them. Whether you're the host or the guest, it's really up to you to make the other person look good. To be completely honest, we're all always trolling for business, but it has to be the right fit and it can never dilute the value of the interview or topic.

"It's truly about value and not the size of the audience. For example, if you have a podcast about business and manage to snag a big celebrity for your show, how does it serve your audience? For example, if you manage to book Tom Cruise for an interview on your business-related podcast, what does that do other than give you some bragging rights? How does it benefit your audience? How does it help you deliver value to your audience? The better guest would be someone who's unknown who's doing two million dollars from their basement with low to no overhead and is tearing it up because they have great skills. I would much rather interview that person because they'll help my audience and me grow our businesses."

Get beyond the mindset that podcasts are simply publicity so you have to be in front of the biggest audience as possible. That is not the way to grow your business and use podcasts as a marketing vehicle. You have to be in front of the right audience, not a big audience, and connect with the host. You must also have the back end ready to go. Your website has to be great, and you'll want to stay in touch with the host to deepen the relationship you start during the initial interview. It's all about relationships and has little, if anything, to do with the size of the audience.

The Million-Dollar Platform

Another thing Jim teaches is something he calls "The Million-Dollar Platform." If you want to grow a profitable business and reach six figures, seven figures, and beyond, you should be marketing on all different platforms. I've been called a marketing machine because I fully embrace this thinking. Besides my podcast, I also do weekly videos on my Interview Connections TV, write a blog, send weekly emails, and a mailed print newsletter, so all of my previous and existing clients – in fact, anyone for whom I have a mailing address – hears from me in their traditional mailbox once a month. Plus I appear as a guest expert on other podcasts and network at events. I do all this marketing because I know that people learn in many different ways.

When you host a podcast but do not write a blog or produce videos, you are excluding a whole segment of prospects who may prefer written or video content. You may be missing out on quite a large number of prospects and leads. There could be many people who need what you offer and for whom you are a perfect fit, but they are not listening to podcasts. If you do not host your own show, and only appear as a guest expert on other shows, you are getting valuable exposure to many different audiences; however, you are missing out on the opportunity to cultivate a community of your own.

It's very important for you to be marketing on all these platforms: podcasting, blogs, videos, emails, and newsletters. I want to teach you the importance of having a million-dollar platform as I close this book because regardless of which side of the mic you choose to podcast from, the guest expert or the host side or both, it is all for nothing if you don't have a platform of content for new fans and followers to consume once the recording ends. If you only focus on one aspect (for example, you only podcast or you only blog), I guarantee that you will miss out on prospects, and you never know which of those prospects may turn into your next huge client!

You must always be marketing. Constantly offer valuable content in a variety of forms for your prospects.

I had a client at Interview Connections who was disappointed and complained about how few podcast listeners were joining his email list. As we already covered in the section on indirectly monetizing your podcast, the goal is to get your podcast listeners to your email list in order to continue nurturing your relationship with them and moving them along your sales funnel.

That said, his disappointment would have been applicable. However (and this is a *huge* however), when I visited his website to see why people were not opting in, the answer quickly became glaringly obvious! The website had *zero* content. No blog posts to read, no videos to watch, or no other podcasts to listen to. There was only an opt-in form that read, "Join my community!" Where's the value in that?!

We're all incredibly busy and don't have time to take a chance opting in to something about which we know little or nothing. Most entrepreneurs today are in a ton of communities. They are participating in multiple Facebook groups and LinkedIn forums and receive hundreds of emails per week. However, they don't agree to those until they have a clear understanding about how the community, group, or forum will provide value to them.

If you don't provide other content to support your expertise and to offer additional value to podcast listeners, you will be as disappointed as my client... and with no one to blame but yourself. You must have a broad platform to create a million-dollar business. Look to any successful entrepreneur and that is exactly what you will find: multiple channels that are reaching prospects, customers, and clients on many levels and in the way they prefer.

Three Reasons to Start a Podcast

When I look at my client base, clearly there are more entrepreneurs who want to be podcast guest experts than host their own shows. Admittedly, it's far easier to be a guest than to tackle hosting your own podcast with all of the steps needed to record, edit, publish, and promote your show.

Which should you do first? Be a podcast guest expert or host your own podcast? Ideally, as I mentioned, I want to see you do both – be a guest and host as a way to market and grow your business. But I do think that if you are truly just getting started, being a guest expert is a great first step to get into podcasting. One of the reasons for this is that you can "get your feet wet" in the podcasting world without having the pressure of producing, launching, and marketing your own show. I organized this book (covering what you need to be a podcast guest expert first) for that very reason.

You can also begin to build your network. As a podcast guest expert, every time you're interviewed, you're connecting with and starting a relationship with another podcaster and another entrepreneur in your niche. It's a great way to build relationships. Let's say you spend a whole year as a guest expert on podcasts. As an example, my client, Heather Havenwood (who we book four times monthly on podcasts), spent a year as a guest expert. She did a ton of shows and she was on a variety of podcasts. After a year, she launched her show, *The Win*, and she was able to get a sponsor immediately because she had already grown a network and made a name for herself in the podcasting world before launching her own show.

If you're doing podcasts as a guest expert, you want to be sure to leverage that, but I do recommend that you strive to get to the point at which you launch your own podcast because you'll start to see the effects of podcasting explode and be really beneficial for your business.

So, on to the three reasons to create your own show....

Reason Number One: Having your own show is an amazing way to market your business. While you should be marketing on all platforms, when you provide valuable, relevant content that your audience (your current and potential customers and clients) needs and wants, they are sticking to you. Consider this analogy: Everything that you do in your marketing is like consistently adding glue between you and your clients and prospects. When you keep adding glue to the relationship, they

Interview Connections

stick with you longer and become even more valuable to your business and your bottom line.

For my own podcast, *Rhodes to Success*, I've narrowed the focus to include much more podcast-specific topics (e.g. how to get booked, irrelevancy of audience size, etc.), and I've been teaching a lot more rather than being completely interview driven. I do sprinkle in guest comments on relevant topics, but the show is now primarily me teaching listeners what they need to know about podcasting. As a result, my audience and download stats have grown. With that, my business is also growing. Listeners are learning more about Interview Connections and how it ties into everything I'm teaching. They're interested in the topic, listening to me every week for 30 minutes, so they're determining that they want to engage me even more and use my services.

Hosting you own podcast is simply a great way to market your business.

Gene Hammett, host of *Leaders in the Trenches,* shared similar experiences: "I'll make no apology that I am using this platform to grow my business. I put it together to bring clients into my business who might not be reading my blogs or hearing me speak at conferences. It's worked really well. I thought it would take about six months, but I got my first client as a result within three months. After I spoke at Podcast Movement, I had a rush of people coming to me. It was a turning moment and became the fuel for me to keep publishing and keep it fresh. Speaking is still my top lead source when I'm in the room and connecting with people, but I'm now bringing stories from the podcast to that conversation. It has increased my own authority level because the people I'm interviewing see me as a peer, not just a 'fan boy.'"

Podcasting is an awesome way to market your own business!

As I've said, to see your podcast enable you to successfully market your business, you do have to stick with it. It is definitely a long-term strategy. While Gene enjoyed success relatively quickly, that may be the exception. You cannot start a podcast and expect bells and whistles to go off a few months later. You have to stick with it. It took me about six months until I felt like I was getting the hang of it. It takes time to figure out the focus. Even Gene took several months to figure out what type of interviewee was best for his show. The more targeted he became with the type of guests he wanted, the more traction and success his show gained.

You may start your podcast with one focus only to discover that your message is really resonating with a different or more narrowly focused audience. When that happens, don't be afraid to shift direction a bit and direct the topic or guest experts to specifically address the audience with whom you are garnering the most success.

Another example of entrepreneurial success with podcasting is Brad Baldridge. Brad hosts *Taming the High Cost of College*. He's a financial planner for parents who are facing tuition bills and trying to save to send their children to college. To start, Brad has named his podcast really, really well. Prospective listeners know exactly what they're going to hear. While Brad has a variety of guests on his show who address many different aspects of going to college, he is the financial planning expert when it comes to paying the tuition bill. He maintains his level of authority and ultimately, that drives his core business.

Reason Number Two: Position yourself as the authority. Gene and Brad are both great examples of this. When you host your own podcast, you are positioning yourself as an authority in your niche and with your listeners and community. In my industry and as a guest-booking enterprise, I'm one of the few owners of a guest-booking agency who also has a podcast (as well as my blog, TV show, etc.) that discusses this very topic. You can have a lot of competition in your industry, but if you have a podcast and the other marketing platforms that go with it, you will automatically set yourself apart as the authority, and every time you create a new piece of content, that will drive search results. In my own case, when a prospect searches for podcast guest booking, they'll find Interview Connection *plus* my podcasts on the topic, my blogs, my videos, etc. You will attract people to you as the authority and expert as a result of the content you publish.

I interviewed Mike Saunders on *Rhodes to Success* about being an authority figure, and he underscored the importance of positioning yourself both as an authority and also a celebrity in your niche. Some people are uncomfortable with this, especially in creating celebrity around themselves, because of the ego needed to do so. However, here's how Mike explained why this is so important: "Dan Kennedy is a really great thought leader in the world of marketing, and he has addressed this very topic saying, 'If you are not systematically or rapidly establishing yourself as a celebrity – at least to your clientele and target market – you are asleep at the wheel, ignoring what is fueling the entire economy around you, neglecting development of a measurably valuable asset which is you.' In other words, we need to remind our audience what we are doing.

"When you visit websites and see sections for 'Careers' or 'Press,' this is exactly what they are doing. You could wait around for years for the media to maybe notice you or you can have others see you now as the expert because the media is talking about you today. You don't have to wait for CNN to call. Regional publications or being interviewed on a podcast can be the catalyst. Perhaps not much happens when you are interviewed on either of these platforms, so guess what? Your work starts: You have to take these pieces of content – that are your assets – and use them in your own promotion. I call it a 'humble brag' and use it on social media or push it out to your email list. All of the sudden, people think, consciously or subconsciously, 'Hey, that person has some things happening.' And down the road, when you bring up your product or service, they are going to sit up and take notice."

Podcasts are amazing authority-positioning tools... even if you don't have any listeners. Another client had no audience when he started, but he built out his entire platform, and shortly after he launched, he quickly became the go-to guy in his niche.

There is no better way to establish yourself as an authority than with your own podcast.

You will also establish yourself as an authority by sharing your content (i.e. the link to an episode) in online forums and social media groups. When working to get more listeners and build an audience, the content becomes a valuable resource. When you're following these forums and groups, you'll often see the same questions being posed. If you happen to do a show on that topic, you're instantly the authority. Share a link to the episode rather than write paragraphs about it as the answer. It's far more powerful than a simple comment.

Reason Number Three: When you host a podcast, you have a platform and space in which you can bring exposure to your community and clients. As the host, you can interview the people with whom you want to create or deepen a relationship. It's very powerful to actually interview your clients and introduce them to your community. Jim Palmer does this very successfully in his coaching program. One of the benefits of being his coaching client is that he will invite you to be interviewed on his show, *Stick Like Glue Radio*. He'll also be on your podcast and is marketing to 20,000 other entrepreneurs. I've done the same thing and have had my own clients as guests on *Rhodes to Success*, and it's a great way for us to get to know each other better and create a relationship outside the booking network.

You can also bring listeners on your podcast as the interviewee. Glenn the Geek does this on his *Horse Radio*

Network, featuring the "year of the listener." When you are a listener and then hear your own voice on the show, it's really, really cool. It's fun for listeners to hear their own voices. One of my own listeners commented directly how it was really cool to be on the show after having been a listener for quite some time. Interviewing your own listeners is the perfect way to deepen your relationship with them. It's also a great way to have an impact on your subscribers: focus on them. Focus on retaining your listeners rather than always focusing on trying to get new listeners. Your listeners will definitely tell others about it, and that's how you'll grow your audience and increase your number of downloads.

I want to bring exposure to my listeners because they are the most important part of my podcast.

Get beyond being only a podcast guest expert. Step out of your comfort zone and develop your own show to build more relationships with people and to build and bring exposure to your own community.

Never, Never, Never Give Up

With a nod to Winston Churchill, the most important advice I can give you about podcasting is "Never, never, never give up."

There are plenty of entrepreneurs who have tried something in marketing and gave up too soon because they thought it wasn't working. "I tried that and it didn't work." Or "It wasn't a good fit." Or "I didn't have enough downloads to make it worth it." Or "Nobody was watching my show." Or... whatever any of the many excuses you can pick about why you quit. I'll point out the BS on all of those excuses because that's what it is!

Don't be distracted by the next bright, shiny object that comes along. Don't give up on something too quickly because you expected immediate results. If you want to grow your business, you must always be marketing on multiple platforms. Even if your podcast may only have five listeners, those five people are listening to you, receiving value from you, and could well become your next huge client.

At Interview Connections, we have some clients who after four or five interviews think about giving up because they are not convinced it's working to grow their businesses. That is not a good mindset! It's not a good mindset for podcasting or any other type of marketing you are doing. Marketing is marketing, and it never ends. You have to keep doing it as long as you want to be growing a successful business.

Having covered all of the many factors that go into podcasting success whether it's as a podcast guest expert or hosting your own show, there is only one thing you need to do to rock the podcast and use it to grow your business. The one thing you need to do in your podcast to be successful, to get more downloads, positive reviews and ratings is to stay committed and stick with it for the long haul. You have to be committed to your podcast and don't give up!

If you look at the top, "What's Hot" iTunes podcasts in any category, you will see that they have been publishing episodes for more than six months or a year and have more than 100 episodes. They are doing really well because they are sticking with it. I assure you, they weren't doing that well in the beginning and weren't enjoying any sort of download success on episode one. They simply stuck with it. You don't have to be the best, but you do have to be consistent.

Never give up. Be consistent and stick with it. Those two things breed the most success for podcasts.

I started podcasting in the fall of 2014, and at least six months went by before I heard anyone reach out to me regarding my podcast. After a year and a half, I know I have listeners who listen to and share every single show. They leave reviews and share episodes on their own social media platforms. I didn't give up. You have to stick with it!

Yes, podcasting is a great way to market and grow your business for the long haul. You will be successful with podcasting if you simply commit to quality and commit to sticking with it. Keep those two things in the forefront of your mind, and you will be rockin' the podcast from either – or both! – sides of the mic!

#ROCKTHEPODCAST Recap:

- *Once you've invested time and resources to be either a podcast guest expert or host of your own show, it makes perfect sense to leverage your efforts by participating on both sides of the mic.*

- *It's not true that "everyone is listening to podcasts." In fact, most audiences are very small, but they're also very targeted and niched, and therein lies the secret of success!*

- *Don't get too hung up on download stats. They are not public and are no guarantee of success.*

- *Size truly doesn't matter. You can generate a lot of traction to grow your business simply by being in front of an audience that mirrors your business's target audience.*

- *Whether you're the guest expert or the host, the best thing you can do to create a successful, quality show is to make the other person look good.*

- *To market successfully, you must create a million-dollar platform and provide value and content across the board with podcasts, blogs, your website, videos, etc. If you don't have the back end ready for prospects when you finish the recording, you will not get the results you want.*

- *There are three great reasons to have your own show: It's an awesome way to market your business, you position yourself as an authority, and you can bring exposure to your clients, listeners, and community.*

- *Never, never, never give up. Always be marketing to grow your business.*

RESOURCES

An Interview with Adrion Porter on *Rhodes to Success* "How to Book Podcast Guests"

Jessica Rhodes:

Our guest today is a gentleman that I met at Social Media Marketing World 2015, just about a year ago. You know when you go to conferences and you're super nervous, you know you know people there, but it's breakfast. It's the first day and you're a little bit just trying to get your bearings? The first morning of Social Media Marketing World, I'm going into the room and by the way, they provide you breakfast there. It's an awesome event.

Adrion Porter, our guest today, came up to me and was like, "Are you Jessica Rhodes? I think you heard me on Gene Hammett's podcast and I checked out your show."

It was like the heavens opened up. I'm like, "This is the coolest thing ever. Somebody heard my podcast and they're coming up to me." A: You should go on other people's show as a guest and B: Go to live events and you'll have things like that happen to you.

I'm really excited for today's interview. Adrion is a brand builder. He's a podcaster, a speaker, consultant. He has this really cool background working for the Cartoon Network, HBO, Cinemax, and Citigroup. He's a super cool guy. I'm real excited to have him on today. Adrion Porter, welcome to *Rhodes to Success*.

Adrion Porter:

Jessica, thank you. I'm so glad to be here. Thank you for that introduction.

Jessica:

Yeah, I'm really excited. When you go up to a podcaster and say, "Oh, I know. Are you so and so?" That's the coolest thing ever. I truly appreciate you coming up to me that morning at Social Media Marketing World. We enjoyed breakfast together. I'm excited to have you on my show here now, almost a year later. This is long overdue.

Adrion:

It was my pleasure. I tell you that was actually my first time at Social Media Marketing World.

Jessica:

Me too.

Adrion:

I would have never known that because you were so into what you do. I went there and you're right. I heard your interview on a couple of podcasts actually. Your brand was the podcast's interview connector. After I heard it, I thought it was a pretty cool gig, a pretty cool niche that you were doing. Obviously, I Goggled so I knew what you looked like. I saw your content. When I saw you in that big room, or during lunch, or breakfast I believe, I said, "I have to go up and meet her."

Like you said, it's very important, everybody, when you go to events even though you may be shy, it's hard. It's hard getting over that hump. I was there on a mission to learn and to network and meet people. It was my first time. I saw a lovely face and somebody that I knew who was on their game. Thank you for sitting down having breakfast with me as well. It was a great conversation.

Jessica:

Sure. I have to ask. You knew my face. I'm sure you saw my photo if you saw me on a podcast. Maybe you went to the web site, but had you seen my videos by any chance?

Adrion:

It was actually the videos. I heard you, so my earbuds were buzzing first.

Jessica:

Did you hear me talking, just blabbing around the conference?

Adrion:

I first became familiar with you through the podcast interviews. Obviously, after that I looked you up and saw your web site and your videos, I did. I loved them. They were very authentic. I love kids. I love how you had little Nathan there with you and it was great.

Jessica:

I had to ask that because I am a big, not promoter, but I'm a big advocate for marketing in all different ways. I know that if you're listening, you most likely are a podcaster, or you're interested in podcasting because that's what we talk a lot about on *Rhodes to Success*.

I'm also somebody that's telling you go be marketing, blog, do videos, get yourself out there in other ways because you heard me on a podcast, but then you went to my web site and saw my videos and that's how you came to recognize me and came up. If I hadn't done any videos, you might not have come up to me that day.

Adrion:

No, because there were hundreds and thousands of people in that room.

Jessica:

Yeah, there were.

Adrion:

I would have had to figure out your voice. Where's Jessica's talking? Yes, video was definitely important.

Jessica:

I love it. That's so great. You were just getting started on your podcasting journey. What is your podcast called?

Adrion:

Thank you. My podcast is called Gen X Amplified. Think of the different generations, Millennials. I'm part of the generation X, or for short, Gen X generation. It's called Gen X Amplified. Basically, it is the podcast that focuses on my generation, that generation, that mid-30s to mid-50s between the Baby Boomers and the Millennials.

As we talked about early, I'm a podcaster at heart. I love the platform. When I wanted to get into the podcasting game, I wanted to do something that I was passionate about and that was part of a bigger mission for me, which was to redefine the narrative and the brand and to empower people in my generation. It's called Gen X Amplified.

Jessica:

How many episodes in are you at this point? Is it a weekly show? Are you doing multiple times per week?

Adrion:

Yeah. It's a once a week weekly show. I am up to, now, as of this recording, up to episode 29. I'm actually releasing another episode today as of this recording, but up to 29 episodes. The last one was with Brian Solis about his new book, X, the book. It's been going great. I launched last year in 2015 in August. Still a newbie, but ...

Jessica:

Yeah, so you ...

Adrion:

... having a blast.

Jessica:

That's right because you had a baby right around the same time. Your wife had a baby.

Adrion:

That would have been a different podcast actually.

Jessica:

I remember that because I was pregnant when we were meeting. You were like, "Oh yeah, my wife's pregnant too." You had a baby in August. That's right. Now I'm remembering. You had, forgive the pun, but you had conceived the idea of the podcast when we met. Then you were talking about it. Then you launched in August. That makes sense.

Adrion:

I love it. Yeah, right. I'm a marketist. I love those little .... I love that. You're right. When I went to Social Media Marketing World, I actually had the idea in mind. I had not interviewed anyone. I was still toying around with names and so forth, but I knew exactly what the show was going to be about. I knew what the mission was. I knew what the premise was going to be, but I actually was testing out different feedback from some of the attendees at the event.

I hadn't launched. I went there. It was my first time meeting a lot of people that I listen to like yourself, like the Pat Flynns, John Lee Dumas, and people that I really admired in the podcasting game. When I got there, I asked some questions. I tested the idea of the show to people that I met and got a lot of great feedback.

To your point, yeah, it was the launching pad as far as really diving in to this space. After that, I went to New Media Expo. I saw you there again, Jessica.

Jessica:

I get around.

Adrion:

Yeah, exactly. From that point, it was just game on.

Jessica:

You've had a lot of really well-known guests. You've interviewed Gretchen Rubin, who I have recently become a really big fan of. I just started listening to her podcast, Happier, which is a really great show. Jay Baer, I met him and read his book after Social Media Marketing World, Chris Brogan.

How did you connect with these guests and get them on your podcast? You're only 29 episodes in. It's a big feat. That's why a lot of people work with Interview Connections to book guests. When you're pre-launch, it's really hard to get well-known guests to be on your show. What did you do? I know you didn't hire us yet.

Adrion:

Thank you for the compliments. No, it's a really great and important question, especially for your audience. I know you have a lot of podcasters listening.

I would say it was a combination of just hustle, determination, and just having, I believe, a strong brand and a strong purpose and vision and something that people want to be a part of. I will say, though, that your company, Interview Connections did help me ...

Jessica:

Yeah, we send you a lot of guests ...

Adrion:

... during the initial launch.

Jessica:

... of our clients.

Adrion:

Exactly, so I want to make sure that doesn't go unnoticed. Thank you for that. Yeah, I think I had people that I had in mind. Honestly, the events help. I would say that too, Social Media Marketing World, I really worked those couple of days, went up to people, described my mission, described the show and the platform, and asked them point blank. "Hey, I would love to interview you."

Let me rewind that. I didn't ask them, a lot of them, during that time. I mentioned it to them, but I focused on developing the relationship first. Like Chris Brogan, I met him I think it was the first night on the big ship, the big networking event at Social Media Marketing World.

I went up to him. I was already a subscriber to his Sunday newsletter. I went up to him and actually showed him 1 of his emails on my phone.

Jessica:

That's great.

Interview Connections

Adrion:

He had a lot of .... It's Chris Brogan. He had a lot of people circling around him trying to take pictures. I went up to him politely and said, "Hey, Chris, enjoy your work. Here, take a look at this, your last email from Sunday." He immediately knew that I wasn't just some fan boy that was not into his content.

Jessica:

That's great.

Adrion:

I subscribed. That literally opened the door to further conversations, which led to me talking about the movement of really empowering Gen Xers to be stronger leaders in this new media marketplace, to help lead Millennials, to define their story. He loved it. When it was time for me to ask him, "Hey, would you want to be on my show?" he jumped at the chance.

Gretchen Rubin, literally just reached out. At that point, I had already interviewed some really key people. When I reached out to her, it was a cold email. I've read her book. I mentioned to her also that during another interview on Gen X Amplified, that I had with Jay Papasan who is the co-author of one of my favorite books, *The ONE Thing*, which focuses on eliminating multi-tasking.

I'd interviewed Jay. During that episode, he mentioned Gretchen Rubin just in conversation about reading her book, Better Than Before. When I had the interview with him, I remembered hearing the name before. I looked her up. I was like, "She's awesome. Let me reach out to her."

I reached out to her via cold email, mentioned that I enjoy her work. I enjoy what she does with her book, her podcast, and also I had a recent interview with the author of *The ONE Thing*. "He mentioned you." I put a link to it. There was already that connection. Another guest who was a New York Times best-selling author who loved her work, I loved her work. It was easy for her to say, "Yes."

She even mentioned that she felt that my focus on this generation was something very powerful. Again, it's all about being consistent, making the connections. You can find the common pieces of conversations, or if you reached out to a potential guest. Maybe that guest, you have some familiarity with their content, or someone else like 6 degrees, or 3 degrees of separation, try to optimize that. That's what I did.

Jessica:

Yeah, that's great. Those are amazing tips. I have to echo and agree that going to live events is an amazing way to book guests for your show. A, if you have looked into going to Social Media Marketing World, or have gone before, you know that this is not a cheap event in any way, both price wise and production. It's a very big investment. If you get your ticket as soon as they open the doors, the lowest price is going to be probably in the neighborhood of 800 bucks.

You're talking about hotel, flight and everything. It's not a small investment, but the beauty of it is that everyone else at that event also made that investment. There's a lot of respect for other people there because you are all there. You're all there and you're looking around and saying, "You know what? We all made it happen."

There's a lot of people sitting at home right now who didn't want to put the skin in the game, who didn't want to take that risk and put it on their credit card. It's a different conversation. They didn't take that risk and make that big investment. Everyone there has mad respect for the other people. When you go up to Chris Brogan; you didn't meet Gretchen Rubin in person, but still if you want to book people that are very well-known and "celebrities ," meeting them in person is going to be honestly the most effective way.

I also love that you said you strategically name dropped. Not just like, "You name drop and you just said someone's name."

You heard, I think was it Brian Solis who wrote *The ONE Thing* that talked about ...?

Adrion:

It was Jay Papasan.

Jessica:

My apologies.

Adrion:

No worries. Brian Solis just wrote a book called The Experience. We talked about that. No, Jay Papasan who wrote *The ONE Thing*, I interviewed him. During that interview, Jay mentioned Gretchen Rubin and her book. Immediately as soon as he said it, I remember the name. She's very ....

Jessica:

She's very well-known.

Adrion:

She's very well-known. I call her.

Jessica:

She's very well-known in her niche, but then you first said that you heard her and you looked her up. You hadn't known about her before. I didn't know who she was until one of my clients wanted to book her. I hadn't heard of her before I looked her up. I'm like, "Oh my gosh, she is awesome. I love her show." and stuff like that.

That's a really, really good tip is if one of your guests mentions someone in their interview, just in passing, you can reach out to that guest and say, "Hey, in my interview with so and so, they talked about you. I looked you up." It shows that you're not coming to them because you're this fan boy or fan girl, but they've already gotten a little bit of a spotlight on your show. Now you want to really bring your audience them in person.

Adrion:

Not to interrupt you, but just to add to that, Jessica, during the outreach to Gretchen, it was via email, I linked to the show and in the show notes for the episode that I had with Jay Papasan, I actually had a link to Gretchen Rubin. In my show notes I always mentioned key takeaways from the conversation.

He brought up, in the conversation, Gretchen Rubin. In the show notes on Jay Papasan's episode, I mentioned Gretchen Rubin and her book. When she saw that, if she took that extra time, I don't know, just to look at that. If she did, she saw that I was already giving her some shine in another conversation.

It wasn't just, "Hey, can you be on my show?" It was, "Hey, I heard about you. I love your content. I also mentioned you on another show because the guest mentioned you and I thought that your book was awesome enough to mention. Hey, I would love to talk to you more about this book."

Also, I want to mention too, I didn't say earlier, consistency is really key. Jay Baer is awesome. I actually meet him for the first time in Social Media Marketing World.

Jessica:
Me too.

Adrion:
Yeah, he was signing his book signing books, Utility and some other books. He did the big great keynote, Hug Your Haters. I believe that was his first time ever presenting Hug Your Haters. That's his upcoming book that's either out now during the time of this release, or almost out.

When I met him, told him that I was about to launch a podcast, I didn't spend a lot of time talking about it because he was book signing. I put it in his ear. Months later, later on in the year, late last year, I reached out to him, wanted to interview him about his upcoming book. Again, that is a key point. Not just, "Hey, I would love for you to be on my show."

That's okay to say that, but I want to add value. "I know you have a book, Hug Your Haters that's coming out. You are a great Gen Xer, leader, entrepreneur. A lot of what you say could add a lot of value and inspire, and impact my audience. Let's talk about your book. I love the keynote that I saw when you did it in March in San Diego. Again ....

Jessica:

Yeah, it showed that you were there. It reminding him, "Hey, I invested ...

Adrion:

Reminded him.

Jessica:

... in coming to see you, that kind of thing.

Adrion:

Right, when I reached out to him, he said, "I would love to." He did say, "I would love to be on your show. It sounds like a great concept." It took some time. I had to be consistent. He was busy book-writing. He was speaking. I think he does maybe 2,000 speeches a week. He's pretty busy.

After some time where I didn't get any response, I wrote another note, stayed consistent. Probably after the third time, he worked to make it happen. A key point is I remained consistent. You have to be consistent and just don't give up. You may not get that flagship varsity guest on your podcast and that's okay. If you crossed all your Ts and dotted your Is and added value, then there's a better chance it could happen. I was very fortunate for it to happen for me.

Jessica:

Yeah, it's a really good point. I definitely want to talk, just echo that consistency is very, very big. You've got to stick with it.

When I was doing Season 1 of *The Podcast Producers* and that's a 10 episode audio series about the art and business of podcasting. I co-hosted that with Corey Coates. We were able to book a lot of really great guests and also some very well-known guests working for big companies and podcasting when this, again, the idea of *The Podcast Producers* was just that it was an idea. There was no web site. There was no presence online.

Corey and I had our own presences online, but *The Podcast Producers* was totally new. We were able to book really big guests because A, there was a very clear message. B, there was a very clear audience in mind. We knew exactly who our target market was and we could articulate that. We knew exactly what the show's purpose was going to be.

If you can articulate those three things very well to a potential guest, it doesn't matter if you're pre-launch, or if you're 5 episodes in, you are going to be more likely to have them say, "Yes" to you. Of course, going out in person and things like that and having a clear brand, a clear message, and then staying consistent.

You might ask a guest to be on your podcast in the beginning, and they might say, "Hey, not yet." Maybe 5 months later, they have all their interviewer requests in a spreadsheet and they're going back to seeing who they could say "Yes" to.

Cliff Ravenscraft talked about this on his show. He won't say, "Yes" as they come. A lot of times he'll say, "Not yet, not yet." When he's ready to do a bunch of interviews, he'll go back and see who's asked him to be on their show. He's talked about how, "I can't believe how many people stop podcasting after a few months. People that asked me to be on their show, they just give up."

Not giving up is a really, really big thing too of just sticking with it and not changing your strategy. I'm over 80 episodes in at this point, probably a little bit more. I've had the same interviews and everything.

I'm just now .... By the time this comes out, It'll probably be slightly changed, but a few episodes ago, I just switched up and took out the voice over actor in the beginning just because I've going this long. I'm like, "All right, I'm finally at a point where I'm going to change." If I had done that five episodes in and then 20 episodes in, my audience would be like, "What is she doing? I can't keep track of what direction she's taking this show."

Adrion:

You're right. It's interesting. While we were just talking about it. You made some great points as far as if you have those three pieces in place like having a clear message, understanding your purpose, and your target audience. I think that's important as well. I think 1 of the success factors for Gen X Amplified and for me is the fact that I have a clear, defined message, and target audience.

It's very overt in the title. That's important. You may not always, as a podcaster, be able to do that, but for me, and I'm a brand guy.

Jessica:

Exactly, that's your background, branding.

Adrion:

That's my background. You mentioned some of the companies I worked for. That's my training. I have, for close to 20 years, I've worked with big companies and worked on brand development, and strategy, and marketing. For me, having a product on a podcast that I felt passionate about that had a clear defined message was important for me. It was something that came from a very passionate purpose.

When I approach individuals to be on my podcast and I talk about the title, the purpose, and Gen X Amplified, I think 1 of the immediate reasons why they were at least intrigued is because this is something that they haven't heard before. They've heard of Gen Xers, but not in a podcast contest. There are a lot of podcasts that are out there just speaking overtly to Millennials, which is great. We need that.

Jessica:

Yep, or Baby Boomers.

Adrion:

Or, Baby Boomers, which is awesome. For me, I was passionate about helping my generation, which for lack of a better word, have been forgotten, because we are squeezed between these two huge generations of Baby Boomers at 75 and the Millennials, close to 80. There is a powerful story when it comes to Gen Xers, or Gen Exceptionals, as I like to call them. I wanted this platform to tell that story.

When I approached those prospective guests, they felt, I believe, intrigued. It was a clear message, clear target audience, and it was up to them if they wanted to jump on board or not. Again, I was very happy for those who have done that.

Jessica:

Yeah, I think that's great. We're talking a lot about booking celebrity guests. I think that these tips are so helpful. I know listeners are going to absolutely love this episode. I also like to talk a lot about how celebrity guests are not going to make or break your show. You're 29 episodes in at least. We've talked about a couple big names, but I would probably bet that most of your guests are, not to make this sound bad, but no-namers. Maybe most of your listeners haven't heard of them and they're new.

I'm such a big advocate for that. I've had a couple "celebrity" guests on my show, but most of my listeners are people that are new.

Most of my guests are new people to my listeners. They're listening every week and learning about a new guest and a new person. I am such a big fan of that. Talk a little bit about the value that guests bring to your show who aren't those big names, or big celebrities.

Adrion:

I'm so glad you brought that up. It's extremely important. Yes, I've had some "big names" on my show. I'm grateful for that. Every guest from 1 to 29 has brought tremendous value. For some of the names, whether it's Lee Caraher. I don't want to use ....

Jessica:

We love Lee. She's one of our clients at Interview Connections. She's amazing.

Adrion:

She is amazing. She may not be a "celebrity guest ," but she brought so much value. That was probably 1 of the most fun conversations I've had. She is called the millennial whisperer. She wrote a book talking about managing Millennials in the workplace. She has a great company, Double Forte.

Jessica:

Can I just say that Lee was on *Rhodes to Success* as well. Her episode on my podcast was one of the most downloaded interviews.

Adrion:

See, there you go.

Jessica:

It's, yeah.

Adrion:

That's it. I didn't mean to interrupt you. See listen, Lee, after this airs, she may be a celebrity guest. That goes to the essence of you as a person, as a brand and being true to who you are and having great, valuable content. Lee has a great brand. She has a great product. She was a great guest. We had a great fun conversation and we laughed, we joked, but she brought a lot of value.

I think that's really important. There's Lucretia Bracson, who I had on my show, who may not be a celebrity guest, but one of the most popular episodes where she talked a lot about photography, her new podcast, being a speaker, being a great Gen Xer. Yes, I've had celebrities like Todd Henry, who's a great New York Times best-selling author of Louder Than Words, but then I'll have Lamar and Ronnie Tyler from Black and Married With Kids, Jason Swank, who lives also here in Atlanta, who's a great digital marketer for digital agencies.

There are a lot of individuals. I have people from overseas like the Essas, Corrina and Steven Essa, the social media experts and the webinar gurus, Steve Essa. They may not be big names, but you talk about value dropping content when it comes to ability in webinars. Steve brought it on my show. Episode 14. He even did a Vanilla Ice Ice Baby rap.

Jessica:

Oh my gosh, I have to listen to that.

Adrion:

You have to listen. I have this staple on my show that I ask all of my guests at the end, what is their personal theme song? Me, being a music fanatic, it's bringing my personality into my show. It's at the end. It also opens the door for my audience to get more of what the personality is from my guests because I ....

Jessica:

Do they all sing it, or do they just say the name?

Adrion:

It's so weird. They don't, but I've had people sing, rap. It's fun. It's a very fun question. I also ask them about what tools they recommend. That particular question about if there was song that you would describe you, and your brand, and your story that would play when you walk down the street. I do it every episode. I've gotten people rapping like Steven Essa, Chris Ducker, Mr. Virtual Freedom, Mr. U Preneur, I interviewed him.

He and I both end up singing James Brown. He sung Ray Charles. It was great. Again, it's bringing that personality. To that point, going back to the Essas, Steven and Corrina, they may not be household names as far as celebrities.

Jessica:

Yeah, I'm playing this on purpose.

Adrion:

See, I love it, see. This is what it's all about, bring your personality. I love it. That's what I'm talking about.

Jessica:

I should probably turn that off because I don't have rights to play that song. That is the song that came to my mind.

Adrion:

See now, that is it.

Jessica:

You're likewise she playing that song.

Adrion:

I love it. This is great. That's the kind of fun we have on my show. It's toward the end after we've talked about their story and their particular product. We talk about how Gen Xers can be better leaders. At the end, we get into that personal theme song question. It opens a door for just some more insights on their brand.

To your point, yes, I've had the Michael O'Neals, the Michael Ports. Some of the other guests, Lou Mongello's, but some of these other guests that we've just talked about, the value that they bring to the conversation, to Gen Xers who are listening to my show, to Millennials, or Boomers who listen to my show as well, it's still on par, I believe.

Jessica:

Yeah.

Adrion:

Go ahead.

Jessica:

1 of my recent guests who is very popular with my audience, Glenn the Geek, he talked about getting sponsors for your podcast when your audience is super small. He got his first sponsor with 12 listeners. A lot of podcasters really loved that episode because most podcasters are not going to have 10,000 downloads an episode, but they do want to monetize and grow their business.

He gave great content, but he was just a great example of a guest who, number 1, most of my listeners had no idea who he was, but he gave amazing content. I wanted to bring him up because he said something in the show that I loved, "Your listeners will listen to your show because they like you. They will not listen to a podcast if they don't like the guest."

You could have the best guest in the world, or have the biggest celebrities, but if the host is annoying, or they don't like the host, they're not going to listen. First and foremost, you need to be likable and be a great host. The guests are secondary. They don't make the show.

I'm so sad that we're at the end of our episode. Adrion, what is your theme song? I would prefer it if you sang it, quite honestly, or played it. I just pulled out Spotify. The tables are turned.

Adrion:

The tables, wow. You really put it. The tables are turned. I will say this. I am a music junkie. I ask this question. I have a theme song, sometimes based on the mood that I'm in, or whatever I'm trying to promote. I will say right now, since we talked a lot about my podcast, I will say the theme song to the movement in the podcast Gen X Amplified is probably Don't You Forget About Me by Simple Minds. It is a quintessential Gen X classic. Let's see if I can play it.

Jessica:

I'm dancing. I know this song.

Adrion:

Yeah, it's from The Breakfast Club. I thought about that because I think it captures what I'm trying to do with really building up and amplifying the strength of my generation. Don't forget about the Gen Xers, the Gen Exceptionals.

Jessica:

Don't you ...

Adrion:

U.S. leaders.

Jessica:

... forget about me.

Adrion:

Your mid-30s, mid-50s, you have greatness within you. Now it's time to lead. Don't you forget about me.

Jessica:

Yes, I love it, Adrion. Thank you so much. How can people ...?

Adrion:

You put me on the spot.

Jessica:

You know what this is? I was telling Adrion before I started. I said, "Something I did recently was I threw out all scripted questions. I'm going into every podcast ...

Adrion:

I love it.

Jessica:

... with a blank slate." This is the magic that happens when you do not script your show.

Adrion:

I love it, I love it, I love that.

Jessica:

Yes, thank you so, so much. How can people connect with you and listen to your podcast?

Adrion:

All right. You can connect with the podcast at Gen X Amplified, that's G-G. I'm about to spell it wrong. G-E-N-X Amplified with a D.com. Also, my personal web site at adrionporter.com. There you can also get to the podcast through that site as well, but also get more information about me, read my blog about my speaking and consulting. I consult on brand development, marketing, and even podcasting. Genxamplified.com and adrionporter.com.

Jessica:

Thank you. If you enjoyed this episode, visit rtspodcasts.com and subscribe to the show in iTunes or Stitcher radio. Finding guests for your podcast can be a huge hassle. It's one of the biggest pain points for podcasters. Visit interviewconnections.com to learn how my team of booking agents can find amazing guests for your show and prevent you from pod fading.

I'm just going to record my little clip for the beginning. Ryan, please put this at the very start of the show.

How do you book celebrity guests? Hustle, go to live events, and have clear messaging. Done.

Interview Connections

An Interview with Adam Hommey on *Rhodes to Success* "Repurposing Content and Web Conversions"

Jessica Rhodes:

I sure hope you are ready because we have an amazing show for you today. I am your host Jessica Rhodes. If you like what you hear, you can catch us every week by subscribing on iTunes and Stitcher Radio. If you are an entrepreneur or wantrepreneur or really anything with the word preneur at the end, you are in the right place because this is the podcast that will show you how to grow a business using content and relationship marketing. You know how you hear about successful business creators and internet marketers who have insanely high website conversion rates that build the know like in transvector with their followers, and how the same people have the luxury of spending less time editing and maintaining and more time educating and monetizing? Well, folks, the reason these entrepreneurs are successful is because in their arsenal is a secret weapon known as Adam Hommey.

Adam, founder and creator of Help My Website Sell and the Business Creators Institute has taken his passion for helping small business owners and business creators just like you win at the game of business and marketing and he is putting it to work for you. His mentoring and teaching delivered one on one in group settings and through detailed video help you emancipate the power of information by converting more social media fans and followers as well as website visitors into prospects and customers and simplifying your internet marketing technology so you can get more customers, make more money and make a bigger difference now. Adam, welcome to *Rhodes to Success*.

Adam Hommey:

Thanks very much for having me. This is a road I'm really looking forward to travelling. I'm very excited about what you are doing here and I'm so honored that you've invited me to be part of it.

Jessica:

Adam, it was question in my mind that I wanted you to be on my *Rhodes to Success* because this podcast is all about content and relationship marketing. You my friend are an expert in repurposing content. That's really what we are going to be talking about today. Adam and I are, we are both in a mastermind together. It's the Dream Business Mastermind and Coaching program with our coach Jim Palmer. I've actually had the pleasure of knowing Adam since right when I started my business. He knew Jessica Rhodes before I started Interview Connections. You've seen the whole journey Adam. I'm really excited to now spotlight you to my listeners. First, I just want to take a step back for our listeners who are just meeting you for the first time. Can you tell us a bit about your background and how you ended up founding helpingmywebsitesell.com?

Adam:

The short story is, about 11 years ago, actually 12 years ago, back in 2002, I completed my master's in business administration. That's my MBA from Duquesne University. I had a goal of becoming a training and development director for a Fortune 500 company. I did the usual networking interviews, job offers, the whole nine yards, and I turned down every offer I received. The reason is because in the meantime while I was continuing to hold down my day job I'd also hooked up with one of my previous mentors who at this point owned a training and development firm. I was doing some work with his company. I discovered that what I really enjoyed was that work with his training and development firm and very soon I formed a corporation around the work I was doing with him.

I started picking up other clients and back then I didn't know what I didn't know and I didn't know what questions I was supposed to ask. For basically two years I sat there waiting to find out when I was going to get enough clients to make the jump and when I was going to be able to make the jump so I can get more clients? In other words, get out of the pay check world and take full charge of my own destiny by running my own business full time. In September 2005, I got myself to a position where I believed I could do that. Fortunately I was right. Three weeks later at the invitation of the same client I went as a guest to James Malinchak's College Speaking Boot Camp. Many of your listeners may have been to a James Malinchak event and you are familiar with the fact that these are arena size events.

This is one of the major series of events that you see in the online marketing space several times a year. Back in September 2005, Malinchak was relatively new to the game and he was still one of those guys who was putting 30 people in a room and spending three days with them. The College Speaking Boot Camp, Big Money Speaker and all his other lines have come a long way since then. That just kind of gives you a journey through time and lets you know that pretty much anything is possible when you are dedicated and work hard at it and have a vision.

At Malinchak's event, I met somebody in the hall who owned a company that rendered online marketing support to small business owners. I ended up doing some subcontracting work with them. The funny thing that happened and she told me this at the time is in her business, whenever she brought on people to help her serve her customers, within six months, the people would either be so good they'd be leaving her because they are getting higher rates on their own with their own clients or they'd be so bad she'd wish they'd leave.

I fortunately fell into the former category, for three years after that I owned a web development firm. Then in August 2010, I closed that down and I opened helpmywebsitesell.com which specializes in website conversion strategies and helping you simplify your technology, so you spend less time editing and maintaining your website, more time educating your audience and monetizing your business.

Jessica:

That is awesome Adam. If you are listening and you are not really sure who James Malinchak is, he is a very successful entrepreneur. Adam and I both know him and he was on ABC's Secret Millionaire. He's a big deal. It's really cool Adam that you actually had the opportunity to go to one of this boot camps way back in the day. Let's jump into some actionable content here. I want to talk about web conversions. I know what web conversions are now because I know you Adam and I've been following you and I've worked with you, but I know a lot of people don't know. They put up a website, they put up an opt-in box and they put content and they hope it all goes well. What are website conversions?

Adam:

They do all these things and they wonder, "Where is my million dollars? Where is my opportunity sit on the beach, where do I get to work on my laptop from the coffee shop for two hours a week and be able to make all the money in the world?" The reality is that, behind every overnight success there is anywhere between ten and 20 years of relentless hard work. I'm proof of that and I think most people are. Website conversions very simply means when people who visit your webpages do what you want them to do.

If you have a page for people to sign up to attend your webinar, when they sign up to attend your webinar, that's a website conversion. When you have a product for sale and they buy that product. When you have an event and they register for it. When you have a blog and they comment on it, when you go to a website like the *Rhodes to Success* podcast site and they click play and listen to a podcast. That in itself is a website conversion because that's what you want them to do.

I see so many times people get so focused on "We need to get more traffic to the website." I'm here to tell you, the very last thing you could possibly want for your website is traffic. You don't want traffic to your website. People think I'm crazy when I say that. Let me explain, traffic is the reason why I work out of a home office. It's something I look to avoid. When we think of traffic we think of a large number of people all being huddled to the same place, in many cases they don't even know why. When we think of websites, we have to define our terms. What is a website, what is it meant to do? Is it a landing page, is it a registration page, is it a sales page, is it a blog page? Is it a list of recommendations page? Is it a public speaking page? Is it a media page? Is it a meeting planners page? What is this website?

A website can be any one of those things and more, and one website can contain all of those things. We need our visitors to our webpages who are prequalified, prepped and pumped. Prequalified means we are addressing the right people. Prepped means that when they click on that link on social media or in that email or what have you, they know what to expect once they've clicked on that link, what they are going to find when they arrive at your webpage. Pumped meaning they are so excited about being there that they are waiting for your page to load so they can take the action that you want them to take which increases your website conversions.

Jessica:

This is really great information. I'm just soaking it all in. I know that we have people listening to this and if you are listening and you have, you are starting your podcast or you are launching your podcast and you want people to go to your website and play your show and comment on your show notes. This is all, this is an interview that you should be taking notes and replaying and listening to again because Adam really knows what he's talking about.

We've talked about website conversions and we've heard about your background Adam. I want to really talk about multi-purposing content but I'm a little confused. I know that we are talking about both of these but how do they relate? How does multi-purposing and content marketing, what does that have to do with actually converting people on your website?

Adam:

According to numerous studies and reviews that we've seen out there, some that we've conducted and some that we've read and studied ourselves, we've come up with an average. From the first time someone hears a view, or gets on your mailing list or becomes your social media friend or follower, to that first time that they call you, email you or otherwise raise their hand and say, "I'm interested in possibly working with you. I'd like to learn more about this event or this product." An average of nine months to a year will pass by.

As I said, that's an average. I've seen it take five minutes, I've seen it take five years. Just a couple of weeks ago, I heard from somebody who's interested in possibly doing one of our website reviews, who, I looked him up in my database. They have been a subscriber since 2009. This is the first time they've actually reached out. It really can take five years. A lot of our listeners may be scratching their head thinking, "What the heck am I going to do for five years? What am I going to do for nine months? What am I going to do for nine days to have enough things to say to these visitors and prospects to get them excited about the possibility of working with me?"

Jessica:

You are absolutely right Adam. I've been in business. Interview Connections launched almost a year ago, probably about a year ago at the time that we are recording this in the fall of 2014. I've been in business for about a year and a half. I don't have five years under my belt but I can tell you that I know just for example one of the first big live events I went to. I met so many people there. A number of people signed up with me right away and some people called me nine months later and said, "I met you back at New Media Expo. I'm ready to sign up now. I wasn't ready then. I'm ready now." I had been blogging, I'd been putting out videos, I'd been sending out my email newsletters. Similarly, I'll have people that reply to my Ezine, they'll just reply to that and I'll get it to my support email.

They'll say, "Hi, I'm ready to schedule a time to talk with you." Who knows how many weeks they had been receiving those weekly emails and finally this Tuesday was the day they said, "I need to sign, I need to talk to you." Definitely putting out content, putting out multiple types of content and super is super important in converting. Definitely really makes a lot of sense. Adam, I want to talk about a process that you've created. You've created a process whereby one hour of content can be used 22 different ways. I can't even think of 22 different ways to use a piece of content. Can you go through that model with us?

Adam:
I'm going to have to go through this relatively quickly. If it's okay with you at the end of our interview, I'll give all of your listeners an opportunity to get the 22 steps if they are interested. I'm going to through this as quickly as I can. The first step obviously is to create your content. My recommendation is to host a webinar. The reason you want to host a webinar is because that's going to give you the basis of the three types of content you are going to need to create these 22 different variations. You need video, you need audio, and you need something to be transcribed into words on the page. Record a title seminar or webinar, pick a topic with a provocative interesting title that's going to get people coming to your registration page and converting to become people who've signed up for your webinar. Then manage the event using a technology that makes it easy to record.

When it comes to webinars I've really seen many different softwares out there. I'm not going to get into which software is the best because we would have to do several different interviews on *Rhodes to Success* just to get through that topic right there. Let's just say, pick the one that works for you. We really recommend that you do it as a webinar, the reason being is because then you can have the video and you'll see the uses for the video in just a second.

Then obviously host the events. A great way to get the event hosted quickly and get great content you'll be able to multi-purpose, is to have a structure around it. Don't just get on there and start talking. Have your bullet points ready, have your questions ready, and have somebody interview you and walk you through it, so that if there are seven points you want to cover, they make sure they ask questions of you or guide the conversation and make sure you say those seven things. Now you have your multiple pieces of topic based content that you are going to use for this exercise. Once you finish the webinar you are going to basically transform it into three separate three things. You are going to get the video; you have a video replay. You'll render that into what's known as a streaming mp4 file, it'll play properly on mobile devices because people want to be able to watch videos on their mobile devices, me included.

If you have that, then making an audio is simple, you just use some kind of software like Camtasia or AVS Video Converter or Sony Vegas. You render out the video file using just the audio track, then you have it in mp3. For a transcript, you hire a high quality transcriptionist who will not only type the words into a Microsoft Word document, they will structure it so that you can see the various content sections. This is where spending the extra $20 on a transcriptionist who truly understands the online marketing world and will give you a structured product will make all the difference in the world. I personally work called MagiScript. There are many others out there, do your own research on that.

This is where you want to really look for a high quality product because the further along your transcriptionist can get you, the faster you can do this. Now we have to create the pieces. Using the video, there are a number of things you can do. You can take that same video and you can create what's known as an autopilot webinar. Use a software like the Evergreen Business System. I know Jim Palmer. The Dream Business Coach has a website called higherprofitswebinars.com where he has webinars that run several times a week. They are basically auto-piloted. He recruits members of his know-hows and newsletters. There is knowhow for social media and master resellers of his knowhow for services, using these autopilot webinars.

I myself have attended many autopilot webinars and I've bought courses as a result of attending these. They work very well when they are done properly. You can carve this video that you've created, this webinar you've created into little segments based on those topics. Then you can create optimized videos on YouTube. You can take those same video segments, add them to blogposts on your website and put links to them in what are known as autoresponders when somebody opts into your mailing list and then you send them out emails, every day or every week with links to these videos. It can be part of this nurturing sequence.

The more things you say to them to be able to know they can trust you, while you are waiting for them to raise their hand and say, "Yes, I'm interested." Depending on how much information you've got out in this webinar, you can place the video or maybe edit it out so you just have the teaching segment, whatever makes sense to you, put it inside a membership site and sell the access, which means you've created a product.

For the audio, you can upload the audio to iTunes as a podcast, you can preschedule, you can put your teleseminars basically on autopilot as well. If you use a platform called Instant-Teleseminar. It has the ability to have you upload audio files, tell them what day and time to play and then people can register for your teleseminar and at the appointed day and time they can show up and they can be just like the teleseminar is live, even though it's an autopilot of something you've created before. You can take the segments of your audio and you can create still image YouTube videos. Which means you use Camtasia and you set it up so it displays a still image, just a picture and then it plays the audio.

You can basically market audio files through the video platform of YouTube. You can also take it to Vimeo and Dailymotion and other video platforms as well. When you take the audio and you put it with the transcript, you can make it into an information product that you can sell at a very reasonable rate as an entry for people looking to invest in your products and services. They can download something and get some knowledge from your right now. If you have a video product and you also have the audio and the transcript, it raises the value or perceived value of that product. You can also use your audio as a bonus for other products that you are selling and that your friends are selling. Let's look at the transcript for a moment.

By transcript, as I said, you send the audio file to a transcriptionist who will then type it out into a Word document. Here are some of the things you can do with that transcript. You can find your seven to ten topics or subject areas, you can carve those out, do some light editing and that's seven to ten blogposts. That's probably for many people a month's worth of content marketing. You can take each blogpost and you can adapt into a script for a video on YouTube, an audio on iTunes. You can use it for your Ezine or your electronic newsletter. You can use it as the feature article. If you tell stories inside your transcript, you can use those for the personal note of your Ezine, if you can't think of anything else to say. Each blog topic post can be a conversation starter for LinkedIn and Facebook discussion groups.

You can use the transcript to find social media status updates. I've seen people get 30, 40, even 50 out of a one-hour transcript. You can also take the transcript and turn it into a book on Amazon Kindle. You can take four or five of your transcripts, put them together, do some editing and now you can have a published book, which sets you up as a market authority. You can use a transcript to create your industry shocking PDF special report to get people on your mailing list.

You can use it as a foundation for your signature talk from the stage or on podcasts. It can service the notes when you present the same evergreen topic on any teleseminars, webinars, Google hangouts, podcasts you are interviewed on. You can also take the transcript and you can edit it into a series of autoresponders that automatically touch your subscribers and keep in contact with them and help be able to know they can trust you, so they raise their hand and express interest in doing business with you. As I said, I needed to go through that very quickly but at the end of this if you are willing, I'm more than happy to make it easy for your subscribers to get a copy of these.

Jessica:

Yes, definitely, because what I was just going to say Adam is for those joining us today on the podcast, I want everyone to then just rewind about ten or 15 minutes and listen to that again at high speed, because there was so much actionable content in there. If you implement what Adam is talking about right now, you are going to have all of your different platforms of content marketing are going to be filled. You are going to have podcast, you are going to have video, you are going to have blogs, you are going to have Ezines, you are going to have webinars, you are going to have teleseminars.

I hear too many people, too many entrepreneurs, especially podcasters, because I work with a lot of podcasters at interviewconnections.com. They only want to podcast because that's what they enjoy most and that's what just comes naturally. That's fine but take your podcast, repurpose it, have it transcribed, put it on YouTube with a static image. There is so much you can do to reach people through different platforms. Be sure to really

Resources

pay attention to this episode because really this is what *Rhodes to Success* is all about. It's using content and relationship marketing and content means more than just podcasting, it means more than just video marketing. It's using it in all different ways. Adam if people want to get that from you, how can they do that?

Adam:

There are actually a couple of different ways. I'm going to leave it to your audience's own decisions on this. One way to do it is to go www.businesscreatorsinstitute.com sign up for the Business Creators' Institute, the entry level is free, where you'll find hours and hours of training programs like this where we cover website conversions, copywriting, media and publicity. We have the organized library of our Tuesday technology tips and many other things. Once you join the Business Creators' Institute, send me a quick email adamh@helpmywebsitesell.com and say that you listened to the *Rhodes to Success* podcast and you would like a copy of the slides on organic multi-purposing and we'll be happy to send those to you.

Another way is to go to www.schedulewithadam.com and if you want to spend a moment for us to get to know each other in our businesses and look for ways we can support each other, I'm happy to spend a few moments with anybody who follows *Rhodes to Success*. Be sure to clearly identify that you heard about us on *Rhodes to Success*. When we do our call, I will email the slides over to you.

Jessica:

Thank you so much Adam. I really just want to emphasize, to those of you listening to this and your head might be spinning and you are thinking, "There is so much I need to be doing that I'm not doing. I'm not getting most on my content." Again, listen to this episode again, check out the show notes at RTS as in *Rhodes to Success*, rtspodcast.com/Adam. That's where we are going to have really well-written show notes describing and outlining all this.

If you are somebody that prefers to read, we will have this all outlined in the show notes for you to look through. Don't worry about taking notes now. Just check out the show notes at rtspodcast.com/Adam. Again, I mentioned that I have known Adam for a long time. I know the type of work that he does and he works with my coach, Jim Palmer, and I just know the work that he does is really effective, especially Adam, I know that you work with a lot of coaches and business coaches, what other kinds of entrepreneurs have you really had a lot of success with?

Adam:

That is one of the core businesses that we work with, we've been doing a lot more work lately with business coaches. We've been doing a little bit of work with coaching and consulting organizations who serve corporate audiences. We've been branching out to a certain degree. Originally it was all primarily information marketers but we are starting to branch out in some of those other areas. As far as business size, we typically work with the small to mediums. We find out that's where we can get the best results the fastest.

I would also suggest that regardless of where you are on the success continuum, whether you are just starting out or whether you've already achieved a certain level of success and you want to take it to the next level or take it to a new direction, that you certainly consider that we should have a conversation about how that can work out for you, because I think that there are a lot of different ways we can work together. I also believe that there is something for everybody, lets figure that out.

Jessica:

I can't emphasize enough the importance of when you are growing your coaching business or your consulting business or whatever business it might be. When you want to take things to the next level, it's really important that you invest in someone like Adam who has the brilliant mind that knows how to get into the backend of what's going behind your website and just really implement systems that increase your conversion rates that help you multi-purpose content.

I've just, because we both work with Jim Palmer. I have seen a lot of behind-the-scenes work on what he does. The little things he changes with certain forms or with how people are getting into their sales funnel and how they are, there is so much that I probably can't even really put into the right words. I just want to encourage you to check Adam out. Adam also has a podcast, an internet radio show. Adam, if people want to listen to that show and hear more of your voice, where can they listen?

Adam:

businesscreatorsradioshow.com

Jessica:

Again, Help My Website Sell, businesscreatorsradioshow.com. We will link up to all of this in the show notes at rtspodcast.com/Adam. Adam are there any final words of wisdom you'd like to leave *Rhodes to Success* with?

Adam:

I'd like to leave just one final thing. I know we had a limit in the amount of time today. There is this one more thing I want to say. Folks get concerned when they create their content that they've said this all before, that it's really nothing new in the marketplace or it's starting to get boring. What I'd like to leave you with is the thought that just when it starts to get boring for you, may very well be the point where it starts to get really interesting for somebody who's been listening to you. Whether they've been listening for three days, three months or three years. This might be the day they are ready to hear your message. Don't give up, make sure you multi-purpose, make sure you continue to be persistently consistent with your website conversion conversation. The results will come when you are dedicated.

Jessica:

Adam gave me that exact feedback on a mastermind call a couple of months ago when I was having the same challenge of,

"I've been doing videos, I've been blogging. I've been doing my conference calls, my group coaching calls. I'm not sure there is anything more to talk about." Adam said exactly that and he's absolutely right, because there is, whether you've given the same tip a million times, there is always a different spin on it. There is always new people finding you and there is always, people don't remember everything you say. Thank you so much Adam. This was so helpful. It was great for me to just hear it and be reminded of all the different ways I can be multi-purposing my content. Again, check out Adam at businesscreatorsinstitute.com and helpmywebsitesell.com. businesscreatorradioshow.com did I get that right?

Adam:

businesscreatorsradioshow.com you should be very proud Jessica. You were our very first live guest.

Jessica:

Yes, I was. I was interviewed on the radio show. You can check that out everyone. Again, we are going to link up to this all in the show notes at rtspodcast.com. Thank you so much for joining us today Adam. If you enjoyed this episode, visit rtspodcast.com and subscribe to the show in iTunes or Stitcher Radio. *Rhodes to Success* is a production of Interview Connections where we book great podcast guests visit interviewconnections.com to learn more about how we can help you start or grow your podcast.

Resources

ABOUT THE AUTHOR –

Jessica Rhodes is the founder and CEO of InterviewConnections.com, the premier guest-booking agency for podcasters and guest experts! After starting her own virtual assistant business, Entrepreneur Support Services, Inc., where she got her clients booked for interviews one on one, she realized there was a real need in the podcasting industry for a premier connector of hosts and great guests! In September 2013, Jessica launched Interview Connections, and today she and her team of highly trained and skilled booking agents personally represent both podcast hosts and guest experts. As a team, they book hundreds of interviews every month.

Jessica **knows** the podcasting industry. She is the host of the hit weekly web TV show, *Interview Connections TV* where she helps you #ROCKTHEPODCAST from **both** sides of the mic! Jessica is also the host of *Rhodes to Success*, a weekly podcast that teaches you strategies for leveraging the power of podcasting both as a guest expert and a host. She is also the co-host of *The Podcast Producers* with Corey Coates, an audio series about the art and business of podcasting. After just one season, Apple selected *The Podcast Producers* as a "How to Podcast" show in the iTunes store and the podcast is now part of a course syllabus for a university in Canada.

Jessica is a sought-after speaker on the power of podcast interviews. She speaks regularly at Dream Business Academy and has shared the stage with top podcasters at Podcast Movement, Podcast New England, the Mid-Atlantic Podcast Conference and Podfest.us.

Made in the USA
San Bernardino, CA
04 March 2017